STONE SOUP

STONE SOUP

The Secret Recipe for Making Something From Nothing

BILL LIAO

bookshaker

First Published in Great Britain 2010
by www.bookshaker.com

This book is dedicated to my wife Kerrie and to my children Liam, Riley and Willow and their very special grandparents Christine, James, Aileen and Dennis.

Acknowledgements

Many thanks to John Renesch for inspiring me, to Jessica Marks and Rebecca Self for their hard work and to Deirdre Nuttall for her assistance in preparing this book.

I also wish to thank The Hunger Project and Landmark Education for the great input they have had into who I have become.

Special thanks to my mentors and betters John Colville, Martin Harris, Syd Teeuwsen, Neil Sunderland and Holger Smyth for showing me the way when I needed it. Thanks also to Peter Ball, Stephen Moignard and Lars Hinrichs for being great leaders to work with.

Last, and of course not least, I would like to thank Ruby, for reasons that will soon be obvious.

Contents

Praise

"Bill is a true friend, a wise business partner, a part of our family and a brilliant idea-tank for every topic that comes up. Bill will make you think. I have had the luck and opportunity to learn lots from him in many areas. I hope that Stone Soup will give you the same opportunity; learning from one of the most extraordinary and special people alive. Thank you, Bill."

Lars Hinrich, German entrepreneur and co-founder of XING, www.xing.com

"Bill Liao has cooked up the perfect recipe for a life of meaning, purpose, creativity, and contribution. It's not only a book of stories, it's also a book of wisdom."

Alan M. Webber, Author of Rules of Thumb, Co-founder, Fast Company magazine, www.rulesofthumbbook.blogspot.com

"Bill Liao is a doer, someone who lives by his instincts and who has a mind open to new ideas. He has woven his message, to both business people and the rest of us, into a tale that makes us want to keep reading. I also believe we should take life by the scruff of the neck, that we should listen to what people are saying and be always curious, never jealous or covetous of other people's success. As Bill tells us you never know what could come from an unexpected encounter or from taking a courageous step towards what you think is right. It is the things in life we don't do that we regret more than the things we do that fail. The story of the Stone Soup and of Ruby demonstrates what Bill has to say: Deliver on your promises, however small. As the book tells us, our reputations come by word of mouth, by how we deal with other people."

Carole Stone, a networker who believes passionately in bringing people together, www.yougovstone.com

"The 20th century saw the publication by Jack Canfield of a recipe for Chicken Soup to nourish our souls. In the early 21st century, the pace of life is speeding up and we are facing new challenges and need to work smarter. A new recipe is called for and Bill Liao has cooked one up in the form of Stone Soup.

"Stone Soup is full of layered and nested metaphor and is a cookbook that every 21st century business, small or large, should read. Bill's mythical story telling is reminiscent of Paulo Coelho's. His approach simplifies what we have all made complex. By getting back to basics, business can not only survive but thrive by nurturing the minds, hearts and souls of the team. Thank you, Bill, for concocting such a magical and rich mixture from such basic and freely available ingredients."

Tom Evans, Author's mentor, writer and coach,
author of Blocks, www.thebookwright.com

"Too sophisticated and cynical are we, sometimes, to believe that the secrets to success are revealed in a fairytale like STONE SOUP. Bill has been my mentor for four years, and our mentorship started with 'one generous portion of belief' (the most important ingredient for STONE SOUP) that an individual's success could be aligned with making contribution to others. 'Accepting reality, visualizing goals and contributing to others,' are the three keys that Bill provided to me (elaborated in detail in STONE SOUP), and I memorized them by repetitive practicing and internalized them by enthusiastic preaching.

"Bill's coaching transformed me from a hesitant and confused fresh graduate to a determined and confident venture capital investment professional, and more significantly, to a contributor that associates his mission with the welfare of the community. I am deeply convinced that success could be taught, and I am living evidence of the magic of STONE SOUP! All the secrets are awaiting you in the book and, remember, it takes 'one generous portion of belief' in what you read in it."

Weber Tong-Ming Su, Mentee of Bill Liao

"I met Bill when he gave a truly inspiring talk on Neo.org, the social networking platform with a purpose. It was not only this great new platform which intrigued me, but the story Bill had about where he has come from, where he is now, and where he is going. I contacted Bill after the event to talk about ideas for Neo, but knew straight away he was the person I needed to support my business, and myself, through what I foresaw as some of the most exciting and challenging times I would face as a business leader.

"Bill's techniques of working with businesses are unlike any I had seen or heard of in my search for my ideal mentor and member of our board. His techniques focus on coaching, encouragement and trust. He digs deep into your inner psyche to unpack your fears, and 'de-clutter' your mind, and self, to give the space required to move forward. Bill won't tell you what to do, or even give you the answers or try and take control of the business, but gives you nuggets of information. Like a magician, he silently gives clues and guidance and then you can see the magic start to happen.

"Stone Soup is a must-read for any type of entrepreneur to achieve their success and goals in life and business!"

Jude Ower, games developer and entrepreneur, www.digital2point0.com

"Bill Liao is a rare combination of wildly successful businessman, introspective thinker, and generous spirit. In Stone Soup he entertains us with some engaging and candid storytelling and gives us some real access to the source of his success. This is the kind of book that actually makes a difference."

Allan L. Cohen, Business Strategist www.allancohen.com

"Stone Soup is entertaining and contains thematic, powerful lessons for us all. The fable itself is a wonderful yet very practical metaphor. It offers a very fresh approach to life and work…it will do well in the marketplace."

John Renesch, writer and thinker on matters of social and organizational change, www.renesch.com

Foreword

You, my dear reader, are in for a tasty, heart warming meal of delicious lessons provided by Bill Liao, chef of "Stone Soup". Go find a cosy place to read, maybe a dog or a cat to curl up with you, tuck your intellectual napkin under your chin and dig in! Or if you're in your office, put on the "Do not Disturb" sign while you savour the goodness in this book.

However, I think that Stone Soup is actually more like a Stone Smorgasbord. As you read, you'll delight in the varied "dishes" that Bill serves up. Where else would you get a spread of locations as varied as Australia, Switzerland, the Land, a convent next to a community so bereft of civilization that it has no name, a City, a carriage factory and community park? It has a cast of characters who will live on in your memory because you learn through their eyes the lessons of "Stone Soup": everyone belongs, everyone makes a difference and it's the wise leader who can see the forest for the trees, or in this instance, the soup from the stones.

Bill skilfully cooks us up a tale that stirs in three important narratives: his own life as an agent of change, a pioneer of social and green entrepreneurship; the age-old, well-loved story of "Stone Soup" within different contexts; and the story of Ruby, Bill's doppelganger in the world of creating lemonade from lemons.

Bill is a true modern man, unfettered by archaic 20th century notions of the "proper" place for women and men. Bill invites us to produce, harvest, prepare as well as serve shoulder to shoulder with him and sit at the table too. He listens to us deeply at our mutual table. This is ground-breaking in the world because it is only through the partnership of men and women that we will be able to really transform our families and communities, as well as our globe.

Thank goodness for Bill and the other Bills in this world. Thank you, Bill, for standing shoulder to shoulder with the people who envision a world that works for everyone, with nothing and no one left out.

Oh, and especially give this book to everyone you know who is serious about making a contribution to the world through their family and work! It should be in every family, school, NGO, government and corporate library.

Ellen Snortland, October 2009,
Los Angeles, California, USA,
www.snortland.com

CHAPTER ONE

The Author Learns How To Make Soup

"A problem is simply a fact someone is resisting."
Bill Liao, www.stonesoupway.com

Do you want to live a life that is richer, more rewarding and more successful – whatever "success" means for you? Do you want to master your field – be it business, community, social or personal development? Are you thinking of starting something new and feel determined to give it all you've got? Do you want to understand and embody real leadership? Do you want to be and do the very best that you can, for yourself, your family, your community and this world that we all share?

If so, this book is for you.

This book is for people who are open to working with others, who are willing and able to recognise their own strengths and their own limitations, and who are prepared to make a real, lasting difference in the global community that is our home.

Growing up in the 1970's and 80's as a Chinese-Australian computer nerd and high-school drop-out, my personal goals were not always completely clear to me. In fact, for a very long time, they were pretty vague and it was a rather frustrating situation for me to be in. I knew that I wanted do and achieve…things…although I didn't know what, or how, or even when, to start. I had a succession of low paid jobs, none of which was very satisfying, and I had the suspicion that I was capable of achieving much more, without any actual proof that that was, in fact, the case. Like so many others, I was waiting for opportunity to present itself without even knowing for sure that I would be able to recognise it when it did.

My very first job at 17 was with a former student of my mother's, who gave me some valuable experience and provided me with considerable insight that would be invaluable in the years to come. My former chemistry teacher, Martin, was another person to suggest, early on, that I might be able to achieve more than the lowly goals most people envision for high school drop outs, by giving me a job in his start-up company. John and Martin both taught me a lot about how they had started their own businesses and how to behave professionally with the people I encountered. They also taught me to be curious and that, with motivation, people can succeed in life by starting their own company and working extremely hard. Although at this time, I still lacked the confidence to truly succeed and the knowledge that I could achieve my goals on my own, I had already come a long way from the boy I had been when I dropped out of high school.

After working for John and Martin, I went to work for Canon, where I learned about climbing the corporate ladder and playing the various political games that one has to master in order to succeed in a corporate environment. I learned even more about what a cushy number a safe corporate job can be and how boring and soul-destroying working in the corporate environment can be for anyone who dreams of doing something more real, more imaginative and more meaningful than just fitting into a slot. Through this experience, I realised that working in a start-up is a great deal more challenging and demanding than fitting into a niche in an already established company, yet working in one's own business is also, I believe, a great deal more rewarding intellectually, emotionally and, often, financially. Similar rewards apply to anyone working in an NGO, charity or other group that aims to make positive changes in new, exciting ways.

> *"People who work sitting down get paid more than people who work standing up."*
> **Ogden Nash**

At this time, on paper, I was doing reasonably well while, at the same time, I was singularly unsatisfied with the way things were going in the realm of work. The real miracle of my life was marrying my beautiful wife Kerrie, who seemed to realise that I had the potential to achieve more and who - wonderfully, amazingly - was there to give me the moral and emotional support I needed.

Kerrie and I were in our mid-twenties when I went to work for a company called Computer Hardware of Australia, which was owned by a man named Peter. One evening, we were all working late in the office and in the course of the conversation, Peter picked up on the many concerns Kerrie and I were discussing, including the impending birth of our first child Liam. He told us about a course he had taken that he thought might help with some of the challenges we were facing. He offered to pay for the course as part of the company training budget, as he felt that taking part in it would improve our lives and because, like all good leaders, he believed in investing in his people.

As a result of that conversation, Kerrie and I completed the Landmark Forum, a three day course instigated by the rather controversial philosopher Werner Erhard, originally developed in the United States in the early 1970's. At the time, I had no idea what to expect from the course. I had never heard of the Landmark Forum or of Werner Erhard and I'm sure that I would never have taken the course at all were it not for Peter's insistence. In fact, I had some doubts as to its validity after reading more about it, yet not wanting to look a gift horse in the mouth, I went in with deep suspicion and my own water bottle, prepared to take in the training with a critical eye.

Despite my initial misgivings, I now know Werner to be an exceptionally direct and yet compassionate person - one of the most compassionate I have ever had the privilege of meeting. He is also a man of great insight, whose teachings, synthesised from many sources, have influenced much that I have achieved subsequently and to whom I owe recognition. Werner's insights - which draw inspiration from many of the world's greatest thinkers, while also demonstrating a wholly fresh, new way to approach one's way of being and of doing things - showed me a new mode of seeing myself, my work, my interactions with other human beings and the very purpose of everything that I was working towards.

Werner Erhard introduced the notion of "transformation" to Americans in the 1970's, presenting the concept in a way that no one had heard before. His teachings concentrated on helping both individuals and organisations to create new frames of reference for themselves, fostering a situation whereby they could think more independently and be much more creative, leading to more effective action and major, lasting impacts on their lives and their potential for success. Partly because of Werner's "humble" non-academic background, he has had plenty of detractors over the years, yet he has many more supporters and enthusiasts, and the great work of various interests continues to speak for itself. Above all, the thing that I trust and respect the most about the work that Werner and Landmark do is that everyone involved in the organisation continually tests and improves upon what they do based on what works through evidence and experience-based change.

At the end of the course, I declared that if what I had learned was at all true, I would be a millionaire by the time I reached the age of thirty, because I already had the aptitude and determination I needed to achieve this goal, it was just a question of tapping and implementing them - something I had not done before, that I now felt ready to do. While Landmark did not give me any actual answers to my many questions, it did give me the start of a very compelling framework for asking new questions. From the course, I took away the crucial information that asking the right questions is often better than having the right answers.

Although I can identify the course as an important turning point for me, I still had to learn many things from many other sources to become the person I am today. I now knew that I could only really learn by being in a questioning frame of mind, rather than by accepting the ready answers others volunteered or assumed on my behalf. Continuing to ask questions, of myself and others, is just as important today as it has ever been.

"Your life works to the degree you keep your agreements."
Werner Erhard

One day some time later, Kerrie and I met a woman named Lolita, who was then the Country Director for The Hunger Project in India, who we both found to be both wise and inspirational. The Hunger Project, of which Werner Erhard was one of the founders, is an organisation dedicated to ending world hunger. In Africa, Asia and Latin America, it works to empower people in building self-reliant lives whereby, through their own efforts, they meet their own needs and create a better future for their children. This is done by using much the same techniques I later learned to use to become successful in business, by mobilising people - in their case, women - to become key agents of change in their communities and by helping people to work at a community level in tandem with local government.

The work of The Hunger Project is not charity; in fact, it could not be more different. It begins by respecting program recipients and honouring them as competent adults with both the means and the capacity to become self-sufficient, given the opportunity and the tools with which to achieve their goals. To this end, The Hunger Project utilises the same skills, abilities and knowledge base used by people who have found success in the business world. People are enabled to do things for themselves and their communities, rather than given hand-outs. The knowledge that they already possess and their understanding of the challenges they face are seen as strengths. They are assisted in achieving their greatest potential by being shown all that they are capable of and by being expected to live up to their end of the bargain through the fulfilment of their obligations and responsibilities.

"The most effective way to achieve right relations with any living thing is to look for the best in it and then help that best into the fullest expression."
Allen J. Boone

When we met, Lolita asked me an inspiring question I will never forget; one that has probably had a bigger impact on my life and work than anything else I have ever been asked, before or since. Before we talked, Kerrie had made a pledge of five thousand dollars, which we did not yet have, to the Hunger Project and Lolita wanted me not just to support the pledge that Kerrie had made, she wanted me to pledge far more money than I had, or even imagined I'd ever have, to the Hunger Project. Because Lolita was a great communicator and very compelling in her request, I really wanted to do what she suggested, yet at the same time, I was quite nervous at the prospect, as Kerrie and I had many more debts than assets. Then she posed the question.

"Bill," she asked me, "who would you have to become to be able to pay fifty thousand dollars to The Hunger Project without suffering unduly yourself?"

Wow! I thought. *That's a pretty big question. I was already disconcerted enough when I found out that Kerrie had pledged five thousand! I would have to become someone pretty special to be able to do that.* Yet suddenly, I wanted to be that sort of person. Inspired by Lolita's question, I made the pledge although, on paper, there was no obvious way for me to be able to meet it.

After I made the pledge to Lolita, while I wanted more than anything to feel confident and assured, more than a few doubts were beginning to arise. Who did I think I was? Where was someone like me going to find fifty thousand dollars to spare? I had been asked who I would have to become in order to fulfil my promise. The image that was summoned was of someone very different than the person I was then. It was of someone wiser, more assured, more confident and possibly a little taller and more stylishly dressed. Definitely, the person in my mind's eye did not wear thick plastic glasses.

Not quite sure what it all meant, I made my way to a small bookstore on the corner of a dark street, where I browsed through the business section. While there were a lot of great books, some of which I had already read, it occurred to me that the most valuable lessons that I had been given in business, and in life, had not come from books, rather they were encapsulated in a folktale that my Scottish grandmother used to tell me when I was a little boy. The folktale was that of "Stone Soup," a well-known folktale that pops up in many traditions around the world. Having grown up with the story, I had often drawn on its lessons and have recounted it on thousands of occasions.

Very soon after all this, I quit my "good" job and started my first real business as an independent business coach working specifically on helping engineering companies to improve their sales. My new company was called "Liao Corporation" and it was a leap of faith as well as a leap into the void. I realised that I also needed help in upgrading my own skills, so I, and my new company, actually worked alongside another mentor named Syd. Syd provided me with a class on coaching, sales format and sales training. In fact, the service he provided was rather like a franchise insofar as he provided a proven, successful business model and all I had to do was work extraordinarily hard to replicate it.

In this way, before the deadline was up on my pledge to Lolita, I found that I had actually invested a hundred thousand dollars in the Hunger Project, twice as much as I had promised. I am particularly proud of these first hundred thousand dollars, as they was invested largely before I had really "made it" and doing that had meant finding a level of confidence in myself and my abilities that I had never reached before. I also learned how to communicate with others in a much deeper, more meaningful way than I had in the past. Knowing that I had been able to live up to my promise meant that I was already capable of most of the things I aspired to. By the time I had turned thirty-one, I had become a millionaire several times over, thanks to my network of people, including the Landmark Forum, Lolita and Syd, and the opportunities they created. All of this enabled me to acquire the conviction and confidence that I needed to move forward, yet none of it would have been possible without the story of Stone Soup.

Many elements in my life made it possible for me to achieve what I did. None of them are beyond the reach of anyone who is capable of honouring their word, declaring it as possible and then taking the actions consistent with getting from point A, where they started, to point Z, where they said they would go. The most important thing is to gather people around you who know what you are about and can contribute. In the pages that follow, you will read my version of Stone Soup, related in the context of the life story of a fantastic gem of a woman called "Ruby" who is a synthesis of the many wonderful women - and a few men - who have taught me invaluable lessons about life, business, entrepreneurship and success through the years. I hope that you will enjoy the tale and I am sure that, in Ruby, you will recognise elements of many of the best people you know. Through sharing her story Ruby is real for me now and I know that there are Rubies out there for all of us!

The Author Learns How To Make Stone Soup

CHAPTER TWO

Ruby's Stone Soup

"…all endings are also beginnings. We just don't know it at the time."
Mitch Albom

It was not just a dark and stormy night - it was much, much nastier than that. This was weather of mythical proportions. The wind howled and the rain lashed down until people feared that their roof-tiles might be swept away. Even the stray dogs and cats had come inside to escape from the rain and wind and, for once, nobody shooed them outside despite an official edict from the Bureaucrat in Chief that had ruled that pets should not enter houses, in case the fleas that they might carry should introduce disease.

Families huddled around their fires and talked in low voices, attempting to reassure each other that the morning would come and the tempest would end. They all knew that winter was coming fast and that many long nights lay ahead before the spring tempted the green shoots out of their slumber. They hoped that the provisions that they had set aside for the winter would be enough to tide them through until spring. Tonight was a clear reminder from the powers that be that nature can be indifferent and cruel and that there are times when all one can do is hunker down and wait for an uncertain future to unfold.

In the bed of a small and comfortable house in a village in this Land, which is not so very far from where you live, an old woman lay between worn, patched linen sheets, her long white hair spread out like a burst of starlight on her pillow and her wizened face observing the world from its place of stillness.

This woman was so old that she had seen more than a hundred summers light the fields and more than a hundred winters spread their mantle of white across the Land. Hers had been a good life, long and fruitful, and now, even though her eyes were rheumy and yellowed with age, and her fingers unable even to hold her own soup spoon, she knew that the time had come to pass on the magical story that had taught her how to live her life in the best, most useful way possible. And she knew just who to pass it to - her great-granddaughter Ruby, with her huge, dark eyes and her vast hunger for life. Ruby had just turned seven and was exactly the right age to absorb the lesson from her great-grandmother's tale. Already, the old woman could see that Ruby was a very special person with aptitudes that were yet untapped and a mind that was as wide open as the prairies that stretched away, apparently endlessly, on either side of the Land in which they had both lived for all of their lives.

"Come and sit by me, Ruby," the old woman said in her soft, cracked voice. "Come and sit with me and I will tell you a story. You like stories, don't you?"

"Yes, grandma, I do. I love stories!"

"I thought so. And I know one of the best stories in the world."

"I don't know anybody who can tell a story the way you do, grandma."

"Thank you, my dear. Now come here."

Obediently, the little girl went to her great-grandmother's bed and perched on the heavy quilt. She looked at the old woman expectantly as she reached out a little hand to stroke the old, withered cheek. She loved her great-grandmother very much. The old woman had always been a touchstone in Ruby's family and it seemed that the little girl had a special bond with her.

"Here is how it begins," the old woman said, and in a voice as clear as she could summon with her rapidly fading strength, she began to tell the tale.

***

This story did not take place yesterday or today – it took place a long time ago when the animals still knew how to speak and before the stars had stopped singing. It was in a village not very unlike this one, when the times were very hard. Famine ravaged the Land and many families did not have enough to eat. The men tightened their belts, the women adjusted their skirts and the children sucked on their leather mittens. Winter was coming in, and people were staying in their own homes, counting out their beans and hoping and praying that they would live to see the spring.

It was at this time, into this village that a strange man came, a magician who knew the limitless power of words, walking with great strides as if he did not have a doubt in the world. His beard was long and wild. His clothes were brightly coloured and ragged. In his left pocket lived an albino mouse and in the right he kept a handful of dried grass, twisted into the rough shape of a man. On his belt he wore a knife, a wooden flute, and a little leather sack. His hat was tall and pointed and his eyes were merry and bright.

As the strange man entered the village, all the children ran behind him as their parents watched with anxious eyes, waiting to see what he would do. This was a Land to which visitors rarely came and those who did come mostly conformed to the strict clothing regulations. It was unheard of to see someone dressed in such an odd and eccentric manner and nobody could imagine what the man's outlandish clothing was supposed to mean.

The magician walked into the centre of the village, turned three times and chose one of the houses. He walked right up to it and knocked on the door. He rapped three times and when the woman of the house arrived she asked him what he wanted.

"I don't want anything," he said. "Nothing at all. Merely a place to sleep by your fire for the night. I will be as quiet as a mouse and you will not even realise that I am there."

The woman hesitated. She was reluctant to let a stranger into her home, especially in these embattled times and this particular stranger looked exceptionally odd. She had never seen anyone even remotely similar. Hadn't he heard of the clothing regulations? How, she wondered, had he even managed to get past the border guards. On the other hand, the nights were getting long and dark and she did not want to be the one to turn somebody away in their hour of need. After exchanging glances with her husband, who sat just inside the door dolefully chewing on a long-depleted cob of corn, she let the man in.

"You are welcome to stay for one night," she said. "I warn you that we cannot be as hospitable as I would like. Famine has been stalking the Land these past few years, and there is very little to eat here. We will not be able to share our evening meal with you. I am sure you understand. There is not even enough for ourselves. Look at my husband; he has been chewing that grainless cob of corn for several days now."

"Madam," said the magician, doffing his hat. "I understand completely. Fortunately, I have brought my own provisions and I have no need of anything else. If you could just lend me a large pot and graciously allow me to use a little of your water."

"Of course, we have water in abundance." The woman took out the biggest pot she had and filled it with the water she had collected from the well that very day.

The family watched in amazement as the mysterious stranger opened the leather pouch he carried at his waist and removed a stone, a very ordinary looking stone, which he

14

popped into the pot of water he was offered and then placed the pot on the fire, humming merrily as he did so. After asking permission from the woman of the house, he removed his wet boots and stretched out by the fire, waiting for his meal to be ready. As he waited, he played a quiet tune on his flute and his albino mouse popped out of his pocket and began to run up and down his sleeve, as if he was dancing to the music. The little animal's whiskers twitched with curiosity as it surveyed its surroundings.

The youngest of the children stopped sucking his thumb. "What are you doing?" he asked. "Why are you boiling that stone?"

"Oh, I'm making Stone Soup," the magician explained, putting down his flute.

"Stone Soup!" the children all exclaimed with one voice. "What is Stone Soup?"

"Well, you see," the magician said as he sat up and gathered his ragged robes about him, "I am a very lucky man indeed. I have a magic stone that I take with me everywhere I go. I just put it in a very large pot with some water, boil it for an hour or two and then I have some delicious soup. Delicious and filling."

"Really?" one of the children asked. "And what does it taste like? It sounds horrid."

"It is really quite good," the magician said. "I have to admit that it is a little on the bland side; apart from that it's extremely nice. It is nicer if you can add a little garlic, just to give it some extra flavour. Unfortunately, I don't have any garlic. I can let you have a taste, all the same. You will just have to imagine what it would be like with garlic in it."

The children's mother, who had been listening all the time without saying anything, piped in: "I could give you a little garlic. We do have plenty of that, at least. It grows wild in all the hedgerows around here."

"Thank you. That would be wonderful."

15

With the garlic added to the pot, the old man continued to tend his meal. Impressed by the notion of the magic stone, the children of the family had gone to tell their friends about their strange and mysterious visitor and by now a veritable crowd of small girls and boys, and even some of their parents, had gathered to see the curious man cook his soup.

A man drew near and peered in. "It looks just like a pot of water to me," he said with some disappointment. "It doesn't look like soup at all." He sniffed. "In fact, it doesn't even smell like soup."

"You have to give it time. It takes at least an hour or two to get going. And it does thicken up more quickly if there is a handful of barley in there."

"I have a handful of barley you can have," the man offered. "While it is not the best barley there is, it should be fine for soup."

"That would be wonderful."

The soup continued to cook. The magician tasted it thoughtfully, using a long wooden spoon that he had taken from the depths of his ragged cloak.

"Not bad," he said. "Although I have to admit that it is still a little bland. It is really too bad I don't have any smoked fish. They would really bring out the flavour of the stone."

"I have some smoked fish," someone offered. "I could let you have a little piece. A little piece of smoked fish goes a long way."

"Indeed it does."

Little by little, the people of the village offered ingredients until a fine pot of soup was bubbling on the fire. After an hour or two, the magician tasted his soup again, and proclaimed that it was ready and that it was the most delicious soup he had ever managed to make with his magic stone.

"What is more," he said. "There's far too much soup for me to eat on my own. Let's share."

That night, the village had a feast of wonderful Stone Soup, soup so good that just the memory of it bore them *through the long winter nights. And the children who had been there that evening never forgot that to make the best soup you ever tasted, all you need is a stone, a pot of water, and the willingness of everyone to contribute something small to add to the pot.*

***

"Is that story true, great-grandmother?" Ruby asked when the old woman had finished speaking.

"It certainly is," the old woman said. "And do you know what else? I was one of the children who sat at the feet of that wise old magician. I remember eating the Stone Soup that night; the best soup that I had ever tasted. And I have never forgotten the wise, merry eyes of that travelling magician. The next day, he left early in the morning, while all the people of the village slept the blessed sleep of the full-bellied. Nobody saw where he went and nobody ever heard from him again. Later that day, on the outskirts of the village, somebody found a little heap of clothes, a leather pouch, a figure of a man made from twisted straw and an albino mouse that ran away and jumped into the undergrowth. It was as if the travelling stranger had vanished into thin air."

"Do you think he was really magic?" Ruby asked, wide-eyed.

"I would think so. Magic, as you know, comes in many forms. And," the old woman continued, "what do you think the story was really about?"

Little Ruby thought for a minute. "That you can make soup with a stone?" she offered.

"Yes, in a way. And think about how the magician managed to make the soup that all the villagers enjoyed so very much. After all, in the end he did not just use the stone, did he? So how did he do it?"

17

"Well...he got everyone to believe in his magic and to give him something small and when it all got boiled up together, it turned into soup."

"Exactly. The point is that no one person can achieve everything on their own and when everyone gives what they can, no matter how little, something wonderful is sure to happen. And that, my dear, is what real magic is all about. So remember, if you live your life like the magician in my story, you can only succeed, no matter how difficult things may seem along the way. And that's not all. As you go through life you will learn that there are many magicians out there, that they all look different and that they all have important lessons for us to learn. Keep your eyes and your heart open to possibility and who knows who you will meet and what you will learn from them."

That night, although her energies were fading fast, the old woman asked Ruby to retell the story to her while she listened quietly and carefully to every nuance and detail. She made sure that Ruby understood the meaning of the story and that she knew how to tell the story well and convincingly. She knew that it was not enough for Ruby to have knowledge, she also needed to be able to communicate to those whom she would meet on her journey through life.

"Ruby, my dear," she said finally, clasping her wrinkled hand firmly around her great-granddaughter's smooth one, "You have the power to achieve greatness. I know that you do and I want you to believe that from the tip of your nose to the heels of your boots. Hold it in your heart, together with me. There will be many times when people will doubt you. They will use harsh words and tell you that your ideas are wrong and your ambitions groundless. There will be occasions when all you can hear are doubting voices. There will even be occasions when the most doubting voice of all is your own. I want you to promise me that, when it happens, you will listen to your heart. You will do what you just know to be right, even in the face of criticism."

"I will." While Ruby did not really understand what she was promising, she knew from her great-grandmother's serious tone that it was important and she was determined to do what she had been advised.

"And now, my dear, kiss me. I have a feeling that I may have to leave you very soon."

"Leave me? What a silly thing you are saying, grandma," Ruby answered innocently. "You haven't gone anywhere for years. Why, you hardly ever even get out of bed anymore." She leaned over and pressed a very affectionate kiss onto the papery cheek of the old woman, who smiled and closed her eyes, exhausted from the effort of telling Ruby the story of Stone Soup.

Long after midnight, when Ruby had gone to bed and was sleeping the blissful, deep sleep reserved for small children, the old woman's eyelashes fluttered for the very last time and she breathed her very last breath. Outside, a bright red butterfly briefly brushed its wings against the window before flying away, despite the fact that it was the middle of the night and certainly not the season for butterflies.

On the next day, they buried the old woman in the cold, hard ground of the local cemetery. Many came to attend the funeral of a much-beloved member of the community, including a mysterious stranger whose bright eyes surveyed the little girl at the graveside, as his long-fingered hand caressed the tiny albino mouse that peeked from his breast pocket. When spring came, the old woman's grave was bright with flowers -

daisies, marigolds and bright red poppies - although none had been planted there.

> *"Like an ability or a muscle, hearing your inner wisdom is strengthened by doing it."*
> **Robbie Gass**

In one night Ruby had both lost and gained; she had lost something dear, yet she had gained a passion. As she grew from childhood through adolescence, Ruby often remembered the story that her great-grandmother had told her on the night of her death and she repeated it to herself, over and over again, until it had become a very part of who she was.

Ruby never forgot what she had learned on the night of her great-grandmother's death. In fact, she started practicing her storytelling the day after the burial. She practiced so hard that whenever anyone listened to her tell a story, it was as if they were there, watching, hearing and smelling everything that Ruby described in such dramatic detail. Ruby made the wise old woman's story her own. Nor did Ruby ever forget her great-grandmother, who stayed with her always in a myriad of ways and reassured her in the face of doubt that she had the means to make wise decisions and follow them through to their realisation. Ruby often heard her voice, like a distant whisper through a spinney of trees, offering her counsel and support in difficult moments.

As Ruby grew into womanhood, she always tried to apply the lesson she had learned from her great-grandmother to the situations that she was confronted with and, in the small problems she had to solve and the minor achievements that she was able to make, she was indeed successful. She had to be independent, as she was all alone in the world. She had been an only child and her parents, who had not been especially young when she was born, were no longer living when Ruby came of age.

Despite Ruby's fierce independence, she was, however, always left with lingering doubts: Couldn't I be doing a lot more than this? Is this really all I can achieve? Should there not be more to my life than this? The answers to these questions, much as she sought them, continued to elude her.

Unfortunately, the Land in which Ruby lived was ruled over by a Bureaucrat-in-Chief who lived in a fine mansion on the only hill in the Land and this complexity-loving Bureaucrat-in-Chief had ensured that it was very difficult - if not entirely impossible - for anyone like Ruby to take real strides towards meaningful achievements in life.

> *"A complex system that works is invariably found to have evolved from a simple system that worked. The inverse proposition also appears to be true: A complex system designed from scratch never works and cannot be made to work. You have to start over, beginning with a working simple system."*
> **John Gall, author of Systemantics**

From his vantage point on the only hill, the Bureaucrat-in-Chief was able to see into each corner of the Land and the loudspeakers mounted on the building broadcast his rulings every day, each hour, on the hour. All activity had to cease so that the people could listen to him speak, because it was deemed very important that everyone remain up-to-date on the latest changes to the law.

The Bureaucrat-in-Chief's life was dedicated to making things organised and tidy for people and to this end he spent most of his time thinking of rules and regulations that were intended to make sure that nothing ever went wrong and that nobody ever got hurt in the Land that he loved so much. Perhaps at the beginning, his heart had been in the right place. Over time, as he grew older and more keenly aware of his own and others' vulnerabilities, he grew angrier and angrier at the very thought of his rules and regulations being flouted, as they inevitably were.

There were so many of them, it was impossible to remember them all, so a book the size of a telephone directory was printed at considerable expense to the state and delivered to every household in the land for easy reference. The Bureaucrat-in-Chief invented yet more rules and regulations to determine how the breakers of rules and regulations should be punished and he published an addendum that was almost as hefty as the original volume. Repeated infringements of the law called for expulsion from the Land, because trouble-makers and dissenters were just far too difficult to be dealt with and administering to the Land was so expensive that there was no money to pay for the construction and maintenance of a suitable place of detention for intransigent law-breakers.

The Bureaucrat-in-Chief banned public gatherings from the highways and byways on grounds of civic safety, because when more than three or four people get together, it is quite likely that they will either cause an obstruction of some sort or have an idea that will get them into trouble. He closed parks and gardens, because there was no effective way of regulating the movement in and out of wild birds and butterflies, any one of which might be carrying some dreadful disease that might spread through the population, with the inevitable dreadful consequences for the economy. He banned swimming, because somebody might drown. After all, whoever heard of a non-swimmer drowning? How much safer it was to simply avoid the water altogether!

The Bureaucrat–in-Chief banned so many things that there was very little left to do, and the Land, which had never been an especially affluent place, started to become very poor indeed, because it was simply too difficult to produce anything to sell, impossible to go into business and too hard for anyone from outside to visit without going to immense personal inconvenience.

Now, even the Bureaucrat-in-Chief could see that there was a problem. It was evident in the ramshackle houses, the roads full of potholes and the empty countryside. It was evident in the fact that the trickle of carriages that had once made their way to the Land from far-away places had utterly ceased, as there was no longer any interest in visiting such a troubled place, where any activities that were any fun had been made illegal. However, the Bureaucrat-in-Chief was set in his ways and, instead of changing how things were done, he felt sure that he could solve the problem on his own.

The Bureaucrat-in-Chief had a son who was the apple of his father's eye. His mother had died when he was a baby, so he had had to raise his son by himself. The many perils faced by children in the course of their growing up had been a cause of great alarm to the most powerful single father in the land and had led to, amongst others, Acts 756, 827 and 928, which banned, respectively, pet dogs, paddling pools and basketballs, all of which have been known to cause injury when they are misused.

The Bureaucrat-in-Chief's son Thorald was intelligent, strong, brave and daring within the limits that were set by his society and his father loved him very much. To say that Thorald was also unkind is something of an understatement. The only time anyone ever saw him smile in public was when he was making things difficult for everybody else. As the son of the most important person in the Land, Thorald had never wanted for anything and it was his intention that he should continue to enjoy this privilege, at whatever cost to his fellow citizens.

The Bureaucrat-in Chief-sent his son overseas to study and, when he came back, he made Thorald a Minister of State, as he was now one of the most educated people in the Land.

"I'm pretty sure I have solved the problem of the economy, Dad," his son said shortly after his return, with all the confidence of a young man full of book learning. "It is tourism. Tourists have lots of money - everyone knows that - and they like to spend it, so the more tourists we can attract to our Land, the better the economy will be. We need to give the tourists something to see. We should get all the people in the Land to work on building the biggest, best Palace in the world. We can live in it, of course, so it will be good for us. It will be good for everybody else too, because tourists will flock from far and wide to view it and take photographs to bring home with them. Of course, once they are here, the tourists will have to buy food from our farmers, clothes from our officially licensed tailors and transport from the League of Transportation Providers and Conveyors. I have already had the plans drawn up."

The Bureaucrat-in-Chief's son rolled an architectural blueprint out on the table and started to point out the many fine features that the Palace would have, as well as the many safety features and the fantastic, state-of-the-art security system. It did not take Thorald long to persuade his father that this was the way to go, especially as one of the few things that did put a light in the Bureaucrat-in-Chief's eye was a clever, grand and complex plan.

The very next day, a decree was sent out across the Land that called for each man and woman and every child above the age of seven to contribute two days a week in labour to building the Palace from the finest materials available in the Land. It was explained that this would be for the good of all and that there was no choice in the matter, because the penalty for the non-observance of the law would be immediate imprisonment and forced labour. Repeated infringements would lead to expulsion.

This news caused great consternation. As things had grown so difficult in the Land, most families were feeding themselves, rather meagrely, from their own kitchen gardens. Raising all the food they needed to eat called for a lot of work as the winters could be long and harsh and the growing season was brief. As it was, they were all barely managing to make ends meet and the winter was a daunting prospect indeed. How would they be able to get all their work done if they also had to spend two full days a week working on the Palace? How would the children learn how to read and write if they had to miss two full days of lessons every week? As it was, they were spending much of the day helping to grow food rather than studying or playing. Everyone knew that the punishment for failing to observe the law was to be banished, and nobody wanted that, so it seemed as though they had no choice at all in the matter. They all knew that when the Bureaucrat-in-Chief made threats, he invariably followed through with them and that they had no option other than to obey the law as best they could.

"You will find that the State is the kind of organisation which, though it does big things badly, does small things badly, too."
John Kenneth Galbraith

Seeing the dreadful difficulties that the people of her Land found themselves in now, Ruby thought about the story that she had learned from her great-grandmother twelve years earlier. She had never forgotten it and had often recounted the tale to herself. Somehow it seemed to be especially relevant in this case and Ruby felt that everyone might benefit from hearing it. Ruby thought about the lessons the story contained and decided that she knew how the people could do the work they had been ordered to do by the Bureaucrat-in-Chief and still achieve the rest of their goals. Yes, she decided, she would apply the lesson of Stone Soup to the problems facing the people. She would tell the story to the biggest audience that she could summon.

Ruby was a bright and persuasive young woman and, at first, she did not find it hard to get people to listen to her, although it was not always easy to persuade them to agree to do what she suggested. When she tried to explain how things would be made easier by sharing the extra work and dividing responsibility, she was met with terrible scepticism.

"You want us to take care of other people's children?" she was asked. "Well, good luck with that; that's a thankless job. Who is going to pay me for that? And what if they get a cold or graze their knees? I suppose I'll have to take the blame. And what about diseases? Children are notorious for spreading disease, you know. I read that they are responsible for 95% of all contagion, everywhere! Children are even more dangerous than dogs."

"You want me to work in a field?" she was asked. "I don't like getting my hands dirty, and besides, I don't have an agricultural worker's permit. What if I do something wrong by mistake and receive a fine?"

Ruby was frustrated when it seemed that nobody wanted to listen to her. She could see that everybody was feeling impatient and cross and anxious and she did not know how best to get her lesson across before they all decided to call it a day and shuffle despondently home. Then, as if from a great distance, she heard a tiny voice encouraging her to share her story with the crowd. Ruby took a deep breath and with the skill she had practiced as a girl she addressed the crowd as calmly and clearly as she could muster.

"I think we all need to calm down and get some perspective. I'm not saying that things aren't tough, they are tough, and I am worried, too. I am also sure that, if we do look long and carefully at the situation together, we will see that the obstacles that face us are not as insurmountable as they seem at first glance. If you will do me the great favour of listening to me for a few minutes, I will tell you a story now."

Her announcement brought about inquisitive whispers throughout the crowd. Stories were rarely told in the Land, so despite the fact that they were breaking the law by gathering in a crowd, the people decided to stay to hear the tale.

Everyone was listening carefully as Ruby began to speak:

***

This story did not take place today or yesterday, it took place a long time ago when the animals still knew how to speak and before the stars had stopped singing. It was in a village not very unlike this one and the times were very hard. Famine ravaged the Land and many families did not have enough to eat. The men tightened their belts, the women adjusted their skirts and the children sucked on their leather mittens. Winter was coming in and people were staying in their own homes, counting out their beans and hoping and praying that they would live to see the spring...

***

Ruby did not even know the word "catalyst," nor did the people listening to her, mouths agape. Nonetheless, she was in the process of becoming a catalyst of dramatic changes that would rock their society, threaten the foundations of the world that had been created by their Bureaucrat-in-Chief and start a ripple effect that would be felt across Lands throughout generations. While there were certainly some people who grumbled that Ruby was not making sense and that it was silly to stand around telling stories when things were so difficult, the story of Stone Soup struck a chord with many more. It also gave them the belief that they could take decisive action to make things easier for themselves and their families, and belief is a powerful source of motivation and focus. Everyone knew that they would have to obey the edict to give two days' worth of work every week to the Bureaucrat-in -Chief's project - that was without question. At least now, having absorbed the lessons of Stone Soup, they felt that there was a chance that they would be able to fulfil this obligation without putting their families through unnecessary hardship. There was no guarantee, of course, that

Ruby's plan was going to actually work. Then again, there was nothing to say that it would not, and no one else had presented alternative solutions. With a plan in place, there was the belief that things could be better than they expected and everyone started to feel more optimistic about their prospects for the immediate future, because at least now they were doing something, and not just waiting to see what more worrying edicts would be delivered upon them from above.

"Management means, in the last analysis, the substitution of thought for brawn and muscle, of knowledge for folklore and superstition, and of cooperation for force."
Peter Drucker

With enough people on board, Ruby had soon organised childcare groups where children whose parents were working on the construction of the Palace were taken care of, entertained, taught and fed simple, nutritious meals with vegetables and fruit donated by all their families. She arranged for the older children to help the younger with their homework. She spoke to the old men and women and asked them to share their knowledge of fruit-and-vegetable-farming so that the plots could be tilled and harvested more effectively.

Because they had no choice, and because of Ruby's enthusiasm and conviction, the people continued to listen to her and even those who had been sceptical at first were won over to her new, positive approach to the problems that were facing their society. There was something about Ruby's zest for life and her belief that, together, they could confront their problems that was contagious. As the people managed to pool all their resources, all the work was completed much more quickly and efficiently than they had imagined possible. In fact, most people found to their surprise that they were eating better, more abundant food than they had for several years and that, for the first time in longer than they could remember, they were going to bed and sleeping the full-bellied sleep of the well-fed. Most families had fallen into the habit of stockpiling ingredients for lean times, and now, in the new spirit of cooperation, parties and shared meals were frequent events. To everybody's utter amazement, they even started to enjoy working on the Palace, despite the fact that they would not be allowed to set foot inside the door when it was built. A spirit of camaraderie quickly developed and the citizens of the Land picked up their tools and went to work on the building site quite happily for the requisite two days every week.

***

The Palace was finished several months ahead of schedule, and it was splendid, just as splendid, if not more splendid, than the blueprints had suggested that it would be - with gilded domes and turrets that seemed to stretch to the sky, wide, gated entrances and gardens with ponds filled with water-lilies and golden carp, and peacocks strutting on the gracious lawns and perching on the gem-encrusted statues that honoured important principles close to the Bureaucrat-in-Chief's heart, such as Industry, Fidelity and Order.

For a little while, the Bureaucrat-in-Chief and his son were very happy in their magnificent new abode. And then they realised that something fundamental had changed in their Land; something that threatened to alter the very fabric of their society as they had carefully constructed it. Even though the Palace had been built, the people had changed their way of doing things for the better and they did not see any good reason to go back to the old way. They had learned how to be more efficient in their work and how to pool their resources and skills so that everyone was better off, with more time for themselves and their families. They had learned how to organise their time so that each man, woman and child could accomplish everything they needed to do and yet still take two full days off every week. Worst, or best, of all, they had started to trust each other more than the Bureaucrat-in-Chief's rules.

> *"Having once decided to achieve a certain task, achieve it at all costs of tedium and distaste. The gain in self-confidence of having accomplished a tiresome labour is immense."*
> **Arnold Bennett**

The Bureaucrat-in-Chief and Thorald both instinctively knew that solidarity and leisure were the enemies of the society that they had created and that they regulated so painstakingly. With two full days every week to just sit and think, it was just a matter of time before the people began to question the many rules and regulations that governed their lives from morning until sundown and all through the night. They might begin to wonder why the parks had been seized and question the reason for the many prohibitions that had been passed; so many that they needed to consult a vast directory before doing anything, just to be sure that they were not breaking any rules. They might start taking matters into their own hands, and acting upon ideas that had started to occur to them now that they had so much more time to think.

They might take to the streets and start to demand that they be allowed to think for themselves as they went about their daily lives. All of that would be very dangerous. Somebody might drown.

The Bureaucrat-in-Chief was very worried by this unnerving prospect. He hated it whenever there was a risk of things not going exactly according to plan. He was quite sure that free-thinking of this nature would only lead to an unstable society full of unimaginable dangers and that would drive all the tourists away – tourists who had not yet materialized. At his core, the Bureaucrat-in-Chief cared very deeply for the Land and all the people in it and it was his belief that he should stay at the helm of his society all the time. Without a firm hand, he was sure that chaos might ensue. Without guidance, people might start thinking for themselves. None of that was even remotely desirable. Somebody might drown.

"Who is the trouble-maker who has been causing all these problems?" the Bureaucrat-in-Chief asked his son. "I am quite sure that few of our people would have been able to come up with these ideas on their own. The 'Let the State Worry for You' programme has been taught in our schools with remarkable success for several decades now and I had thought that we had pretty much stamped out that kind of thing".

Thorald smiled nastily. "It is a young woman called Ruby," he said. "I used to go to school with her when we were both children. Even back then, she was always breaking all the rules, even the ones that hadn't been written yet. It was difficult for the teachers to keep the rulebook up to date, with Ruby around. She used to lace her gym shoes up differently than everyone else, she liked to write with green ink, and she was always telling stories at lunch time to anybody who was prepared to listen. She's a trouble-maker, all right. I think her parents even taught her at home sometimes, as she was suspended from school so often. We will have to do something about her before things get out of hand. Nip her in the bud."

"Stories? Why would anyone want to tell stories? What kind of stories does she tell?"

"The troublesome kind," said Thorald, grimly. "Stories that might make people consider breaking the rules, without stopping to think that perhaps all those rules are there for a very good reason. The sort of stories that should, by rights, be against the law!"

"It is not safe," said the Bureaucrat-in-Chief. "We'll have to do something about it. Why, if I had known that storytelling was so dangerous, I would have banned it long ago." He started to think to himself about how the new law could be worded.

"Yes," said his son. "Somebody might drown."

The Bureaucrat-in-Chief soon arranged for broadsheets to be delivered to every house in the Land.

"Are you covered by health and safety regulations?" the broadsheets asked. "If you are caring for other people's children in your home, are you aware that you will be held liable when they get hurt? We all know how accident prone other people's children are!"

"Are you being exploited?" they asked. "If someone has asked you your advice without offering to pay for it, they are breaking the law and taking advantage of you. Call our emergency toll-free number to know your rights."

"Do you know someone who is breaking the law?" they queried. "If you do and you don't report them, you are committing an offence and that is punishable by law."

"Every revolution evaporates and leaves behind only the slime of a new bureaucracy."
Franz Kafka

As a result of all the publicity that they were being bombarded with, doubt began to enter people's minds. Were they being taken advantage of? Were they, unbeknownst to themselves, breaking the law? Could they get in serious trouble for something that they had done in good faith? Had they all, in fact, been hoodwinked and bamboozled by someone who was just too good at telling stories? Shutters were closed and everyone began to look at each other with suspicion. They stopped taking care of each other's children and working in each other's vegetable gardens and inviting each other over for dinner because something awful might happen in any one of those situations and, pretty soon, they were just as overworked as they had always been, between keeping food on the table and obeying the many laws that ruled their lives. They no longer had hope for a future in which their destinies were in their own hands.

Soon, Ruby had been vilified in the broadsheets and declared a charlatan and a quack who promoted unsafe work practices and stole others' expertise for her own purposes. She was accused of making people work for her without pay and a general public warning was issued, advising everyone to stay well away from the troublemaker. The final straw came when every lamp-post in the country bore a poster with Ruby's image emblazoned with the strongly-worded message that she was to be avoided at all cost. Even her own family and friends started to look at her askance and Ruby soon found that almost nobody was prepared to listen to her at all. She tried to keep her spirits high, yet found this to be very difficult, as without anyone to talk to her loneliness wore her spirits down and left her utterly exhausted in body and spirit. Finally, Ruby was summoned before the Bureaucrat-in-Chief to answer for her crimes. The trial, such as it was, was very brief, because all trials were heard and judged by none other than the Bureaucrat-in-Chief himself, who did not trust anyone else to make important decisions such as who was innocent and who guilty.

"You have been found guilty," the Bureaucrat-in-Chief told Ruby after deliberations so brief that they hardly warranted the name. "And the punishment for guilt is expulsion from the Land forthwith. Take your Form 365 and leave before 18.15 precisely. There is no room for people like you in our peaceful society."

"And don't come back!" Thorald added, redundantly.

With tears running down her face, Ruby bid goodbye to the last few of her supporters and walked out of the Land with her head held high and her heart in pieces. She knew that she would almost certainly never see her home or any of the people she had loved since childhood again.

Putting one foot in front of the other, Ruby began to walk on towards a future full of uncertainty and doubt. The one thing she knew for sure gave her the courage and fortitude she needed to continue with her life and her mission. She knew that she was never truly alone, because the spirit of her great-grandmother was with her now, as always, in a myriad of ways. Her voice whispered in Ruby's ear; *Courage, my girl! Your story is just beginning. Keep your eyes focussed on your goals, work tirelessly to reach them and you will achieve your dreams.*

Lessons from Ruby's Stone Soup

Over the years, I have often been asked my opinion about how businesses and other organisations can best achieve success. Sometimes I simply answer by relating the folk story of Stone Soup, pretty much in the version that Ruby was told by her great-grandmother. I have told this story to a sales team that was divided and not working together, as well as to many entrepreneurs as a way of illustrating how all the members of a company or organisation need to pull together. I explain how, by working together, they can all achieve a great deal more than any one of them can alone. In this context, the story can easily be adapted to explain how you need to inspire each staff member, including yourself, to put in a bit more when the going gets tough. I also use this story to illustrate the reality that participants in any organisation need to be rewarded for their efforts with tasty "soup" in the form of benefits, and not necessarily always in the form of financial rewards, as I find that the lure of cash as an incentive often makes peoples' focus too narrow to allow them to succeed. Genuine and personal recognition of efforts made are also very important and will always be warmly appreciated. After all, who likes to feel that they are working hard and doing their very best, to no avail? We all need to know that our productive efforts are being recognised and that they will be rewarded.

I firmly believe that it is only by being inspired to believe in something and then working together and using all the talents available from many different types of people that true success can be reached. When times are difficult, as in a recession or a downturn, the message of Stone Soup is more relevant than ever. It is at times like these that people who can truly work in a spirit of cooperation will not only survive, they will strive, thrive, and prosper. Difficult times can be tough, however, they are also full of opportunity for those with the insight and courage to acknowledge it and work together.

As we accompany Ruby on her journey through life, we will pause here and there along the way to look at some of the essential ingredients of a really great vat of Stone Soup! By the end of the book, we will have a full recipe for you to use in making your own soup, wherever your life and work take you.

For now, I would like to underline the most important ingredient of all: Belief.

A RECIPE FOR STONE SOUP
One generous portion of belief

In their book, *Waiting for Your Cat to Bark*[1], the authors make the point that human beings behave much more like cats in their commercial habits than dogs. They propose that much of the world's marketing today fails because, with the Internet as their ally, the average consumer is too well-informed to make purchases solely based on marketing messages, rather they are well-equipped to engage in critical thinking and they will only act and buy if they are connected with on a more direct, emotional level. People cannot be led on a leash, as dogs are; they have to be persuaded, like cats.

One day as I was negotiating with a much larger Japanese firm for an investment into our company, one of our legal team suggested that the whole business process

---

[1] Eisenberg, Eisenberg and Davis, 2006.

was like herding cats. This was the first time I had heard the phrase and it has stuck with me ever since. An example of this presented itself in a situation with Lionel, a friend of mine who once owned a small white Persian kitten with a taste for adventure. One of the greatest feats of cat herding I ever saw was Lionel coaxing this kitten to jump into his waiting arms; not an extraordinary feat until you consider that, moments before, the kitten had been trapped on the rooftop of a five storey block of flats and Lionel was on the ground floor. I realised then that love is a much more potent motivator than fear, or as Lionel phrases it - love draws while fear pushes. The principle holds true when "herding cats" in business.

A RECIPE FOR STONE SOUP

One generous portion of belief

One or more enthusiastic catalysts

I feel that I am at my best when I am herding cats in the business world and that these skills allow me to be a catalyst for the companies that I work with. I prefer to be in the background making things work and getting people past their differences than in the foreground giving orders and holding the rudder of the organisation by myself. Some people would call being a catalyst a form of "leadership," and while that is true, it is also different from what we traditionally perceive to be leadership because, as a catalyst, I prefer to follow a strong leader. I have often found that my skills as catalyst have enabled the leaders I work with to lead even more effectively. I have learned that, in addition to leadership, every successful business or enterprise needs to incorporate one or more catalysts because these are often the people who get things done!

At the time of writing, my family shares its home with two cats, a dog and several goldfish. I have found that, with a green laser dot, I can lead all of these animals around the house (or tank) as they are all attracted to things that glitter. Beyond leading them around, I cannot do more with the goldfish as they are not very bright. Our dog, though wilful, readily accepts more complicated commands from the entire family. The cats though, unlike the dog, are always difficult to persuade. Cats, as we have already discussed, do not like to do what they are told.

Long ago, I decided that if I wanted to get cats to leave a room I needed to learn how to speak their language or at least a reasonable approximation of it. I tried imitating various cat hissing noises to get them to leave and discovered that they only respond if you can get a lot of emotion into your hiss. In the same vein, the primary tool of a catalyst in business is emotion. Now, for cats that are in the process of doing evil cat things to prove who really owns your expensive new furniture, fear is a pretty much the only appropriate emotion to use. To get people to work together cooperatively and productively requires a set of different emotions and something more - it requires a clear context.

I see a lot of leaders and managers who get along by using a mix of fear and greed to get what they need done. They threaten employees with sacking or harsh words and entice them with the prospect of juicy bonuses or special favours. I see others who resort to fear, anger and greed when they get frustrated. These leaders do not have the emotional intelligence necessary to build an organisation on fun, love, and the spirit of contribution within a context of productivity. For a catalyst, the entire emotional repertoire is needed and timing is everything, as is an understanding of the power of context. As my friend Alan Cohen says of creating context: "If you really want to herd cats, you've got to tilt the floor!"

In order to create context, you need to put together the right blend of ideas and emotions, and express them in a way that is easily grasped to provide an emotional framework for what you are asking people to do. For instance, churches and mosques often use imposing architecture and high ceilings to inspire awe and reduce background noise, thus creating an appropriate context for religious worship. In business, if you begin a discussion by talking animatedly about your desire to hear other's ideas, it creates a different context than if you say the same thing in a deadpan voice. By creating such context, your audience is more likely to believe and understand what you expect of them. It is much harder, if not impossible, to create a productive context without appropriate emotion; on the flipside, if you do not create an appropriate context then you are at the mercy of the prevailing context which may leave you disempowered and distort the message you are trying to send.

A RECIPE FOR STONE SOUP

One generous portion of belief

One or more enthusiastic catalysts

One well defined context, communicated well

We have all had to deal with difficult people in a range of situations and some of us may have seen how easily such individuals can drag down an enterprise, be it business or otherwise. Bernie, a friend of mine, once defined difficult people to me as "Problem Generators," a succinct term that describes them very precisely. "Problem Generators," are the polar opposite of catalysts. Problem Generators have traits and habits that make them very dangerous to an organisation; indeed, if left unchecked, they can threaten its very existence. As they generally blend in well with productive workers, Problem Generators can be very difficult to spot. Once they have been identified, they must be eliminated from the organisation, as little or nothing will change their way of being, or at least, nothing will work fast enough to undo the damage that they generally cause.

Problem Generators are generally very intelligent and charming. They are attracted to strong leaders and productive people, and their natural habitat is in the vital areas of an organisation. They often appear to be someone's close friend or ally, while in reality they are more likely to be emotionally manipulating other people, usually in very subtle ways. The only sure way to detect Problem Generators is to measure their personal net productivity. It will invariably be close to zero or even negative. Unfortunately, good workers can also become Problem Generators if they are under the influence of a particularly potent one themselves. They can also become good workers again, just as soon as they are released from this influence.

An example of one such situation involves an employee I will call "Jane" who was a top producer in one of the companies I worked with for several years. Suddenly, Jane started becoming difficult and particularly manipulative of two of her co-workers, using subtle emotional blackmail to get home early and to get projects finished as quickly as possible, even if the quality of her work suffered as a result. Her personal productivity went downhill very quickly. I was perplexed by this new behaviour until I attended a social event and met Jane's new boyfriend, Rod. Rod displayed several behaviours that I have come over the years to associate with Problem Generators. He immediately tried to prove to me that his company was better organised than ours, yet he was very polite and friendly in the process. Despite his pleasant manner of speaking, Rod's immediate effect on me was to fill me with self-doubt. When Jane spoke, he butted in to correct her straight away. When she argued back, he would use some of her own strengths against her. When Jane was telling a rather fascinating anecdote about a customer she had dealt with that day he would say, "I am sure that we don't want to bore them by talking too much shop, dear." I could see Jane's confidence and self-esteem taking a battering before my very eyes.

Not long afterward, Jane came to me for advice about her relationship. My response, which has been demonstrated to me many times by my own mentors and catalysts, was to say, "I don't know. Why don't you tell me what you see?" The idea was for Jane to reflect on the interactions she was having with Rod in dialogue with me rather than in monologue in her own head. From what she said, I was able to piece together a profile of Rod that was considerably less than flattering and I was able to point out some of the more subtle emotional blackmail he used to keep her in line and some of the advice he had given her about work that had started to alienate some of her colleagues and friends. We then looked at how much each of them had contributed to the relationship and it was very clear that Rod was getting the lion's share of the benefits and that Jane was paying the price for it.

It was only possible for Jane and me to arrive at these insights because of the trust I had built with Jane. I held out little hope that things would change because Jane was really quite attached to Rod, so I equipped Jane with the only defence I know against this kind of manipulation. I explained that the best defence against a Problem Generator is to see their emotional attack for what it is and then ask them what made them do it. I advised Jane to begin by going home late from work so as to be unable to cook dinner or buy anything on the way home. When she got home, Rod was waiting for her and he was hungry. When he realised that Jane had not brought anything to eat, he remarked that our company was too demanding, subtly implying that Jane's gullibility was somehow the source of his empty stomach, rather than his own laziness. Jane then used the line that I had equipped her with. She said, "Rod, you know what you just said hurt. What made you want to hurt me?"

Rod, of course, denied being hurtful and also dropped the conversation like a hot potato. Over the next twenty-four hours, Jane used the same line time after time and each time Rod either dropped the subject or tried a new manipulation. Jane told me afterwards that she actually enjoyed watching him squirm a bit, even though she still loved him. Those conversations were the beginning of the end of their relationship and, shortly thereafter, Jane returned to her old self and eventually went on to become an executive at a larger firm.

In the example above, a good worker turned temporary Problem Generator by her deeply problem generating boyfriend returned to normal after she got away from him. In a situation with a genuine Problem Generator, the only way to get rid of them is to fire them. Be aware that you need to measure their net performance and give them several warnings, as they will not take it lying down and will often be vengeful.

Part of the problem generator's world view is that they can succeed by pushing others down.

A RECIPE FOR STONE SOUP

One generous portion of belief

One or more enthusiastic catalysts

One well defined context, communicated well

Testing for bad eggs so that you can leave them out

My good friend Ellen wrote to me recently, advising me to check out a recent edition of the *New York Times Sunday Magazine,* which had published an article entitled "The Women's Crusade," all about why empowering women and girls is the most important imperative for global development. She mentioned that the story reminded her of an experience she had had shortly before while travelling in Japan. She had been travelling by train and was at a train station in Osaka, having ridden for half an hour or so in the dubious company of a very drunk elderly commuter. While on the platform, the man started to harass some schoolgirls nearby.

"Leave them alone!" my friend yelled. He staggered over to her, whereupon she held up her hands and shouted, "Back off! I don't want trouble."

The drunk lurched back in the direction of the four schoolgirls, who all raised their hands and yelled, "No!"

As catalysts, we can usually teach most effectively by using our own behaviour to model what we want other people to do.

Both the magician in Ruby's great-grandmother's tale and Ruby herself are catalysts, which means that they are elements that create change around them, while remaining true to themselves in the process. It also means that they were able to change how the people they interacted with perceived their surroundings as well as subtly changing the context in which people interacted to open a new space for cooperation that had not been there before.

I once attended a self-defence course led by a man who had trained Nelson Mandela's body guards. He quietly asked us if we wanted to know the secret of being genuine with people and he leaned in close as we nodded and strained to hear the answer. "BE GENUINE!" he exclaimed loudly and with complete candour. If you are going to be a great catalyst, you need to be able to build emotional connections with people in a short amount of time. If you are not really interested in people and their welfare, being a catalyst is not the role for you. Respect for other people, a willingness and openness to listening to what they have to say and taking the time to achieve a clear understanding of them is absolutely essential, as is an appreciation of the fact that just because someone may disagree with us does not mean they do not have an equally valid point of view. Being able to quickly build an emotional connection with someone is a skill that is crucial to getting things done and it will only be effective if that connection is genuine and deepens over time.

The prospective catalyst has many techniques that can be learned and that, if applied properly, can lead to positive short term results. While many of these techniques can be learned, some will require that people initially take on traits that may be uncomfortable or unfamiliar to them. For instance, people who find it difficult to speak to others or in front of groups will have to learn to put aside their fears in order to truly embrace the role of a catalyst.

While catalysts utilise genuine interest and emotional connections to connect with and motivate people, simple manipulation and emotional blackmail is often utilised in business environments to the same end. Some managers feel that by throwing in a little emotional blackmail, they can keep some people in line for years, though this is far from the best way of building lasting achievements. The problem with using negative manipulative techniques to motivate staff is that if you want really stellar results, you need stellar performers and stellar performers will not put up with manipulation for very long. If stellar performers are treated badly, they will not tolerate the mistreatment long before finding another place of employment, creating more work for the manager in the long run.

Regardless of the nature of your enterprise, to be able to truly motivate an A grade team of people and to be able to build really strong emotional ties, you need to found everything on a set of fundamental principles that you believe in absolutely. To do this, it is imperative that you live and work according to your principles and demonstrate them with your behaviour, bearing them in mind through everything you do. One example of this is the simple principle "do no harm" that has been at the heart of medical ethics for thousands of years and is taught today in medical schools around the world. It is easy to spot doctors who truly believe in this principle, as their genuine compassion is obvious in everything they do; they are the real healers and the experience they provide is the kind you expect from a medical professional. The difference between a master manipulator and an effective catalyst is grounded in the principles they believe in. While a catalyst achieves good results over time, the results attained by a manipulator will never be sustainable. Many philosophers will tell you that people are ultimately motivated by self-interest, so everything they do is aligned with their own survival. Personally, I believe that while personal survival is a strong force for humanity, in general it is at its very best when concerned with the welfare of others: human, animal, environmental, or even when concerned with the welfare of the truth.

I believe in empowering and unleashing the human spirit. One of the personal principles that I have learned and adopted in my heart is that people and the world should be better off after each interaction with me than they were before. While I do not always manage to live up to my ideal of empowering everyone I meet, I do get it right more and more as I become more skilled in really understanding and caring about other people and the world at large. I know that I am happiest when I am contributing to someone or something outside of me because this is good for them or it, and it is good for me too! This is the true nature of an effective catalyst.

A RECIPE FOR STONE SOUP

One generous portion of belief

One or more enthusiastic catalysts

One well defined context, communicated well

Testing for bad eggs so that you can leave them out

A heaping spoonful of emotion and trust

Ruby's Stone Soup

CHAPTER THREE

A Village Behind Closed Doors

"Life is either a daring adventure or nothing. Security does not exist in nature, nor do the children of men as a whole experience it. Avoiding danger is no safer in the long run than exposure."
Helen Keller

Young Ruby walked for many miles, across the plains that stretched out from the borders of her Land, across the gentle foothills that those plains became, up and down the steep mountains that grew from those foothills and on until she reached another Place, one that she had never heard of before. Hers was a closed Land, and studying the outside world had never been encouraged there.

Along the way, Ruby shed many tears and bound many blisters. She had never been truly alone before; hers had been a small community filled with friends and relatives and, even if at times a little limiting, it had seemed very safe and cosy. It had never seemed as safe and cosy at it did now in retrospect and Ruby ached and longed for the familiar with every fibre of her being.

Ruby had never travelled beyond the confines of her native Land before and every new sight she saw was a cause for alarm and consternation. She was full of self-doubt. Perhaps she should never have said anything to her friends and neighbours about improving their situation. Perhaps she should have left well enough alone. There were times when her great-grandmother's voice came to her loud and clear and other times when all she could hear was the beating of her own heart and the recriminations of her own confused inner voice.

At night Ruby slept under trees or in the curve of a rock, huddled within her cape, fearful each time she heard a wolf howling in the distance or a bat flying overhead. By day she walked, endlessly placing one foot in front of the other, trying to ignore her blisters, her exhaustion, and her fears. She paused only occasionally to eat a hunk of bread and cheese from her dwindling supply of provisions. She did not know where she was going and she did not know how she was going to get there or even how she would recognise her destination when she did finally arrive. There were yet more times when she doubted herself and blamed herself for having ever tried to do something new. And then, once again, she would hear her great-grandmother's voice as clear as day and she would begin to feel better again and more sure that she was indeed taking the right path, even though she did not know where it would lead her.

> *"The whole problem with the world is that fools and fanatics are always so certain of themselves, and wiser people so full of doubts."*
> **Bertrand Russell**

After walking for many days through terrain that became stranger to her with each kilometre, Ruby began to see signs of life: discarded rubbish, the bloated, swollen cadavers of dead cats and dogs, maggots crawling in and out of their sightless eyes, footsteps dragging though the dusty ground, the sounds of cooking, of children crying, of adults having furious arguments. This was all somewhat less than encouraging and Ruby did not make any effort to investigate them further. She told herself that if she kept on walking towards the random point on the horizon that she had chosen as her goal, she would surely find herself in more pleasant surroundings. Then she started to pass people. More often than not, they were drunk and they just stared at her, blank and hollow-eyed, before shuffling onwards without so much as a backward glance at the young woman travelling alone.

This must be a terrible Place! she thought, aghast. *What sort of people are these? They are hardly people at all; they are monsters.*

I'm not so sure, her great-grandmother commented inside her head. *This may be more promising than it first appears. It is very important not to judge by first appearances. And possibly there is a reason for the people's miserable appearance.*

Ruby walked through dirty, foul-smelling villages where the children stared at her with hostile eyes and expressionless faces and the adults looked on listlessly, apparently not curious at all about the stranger in their midst, despite the fact that people rarely passed through this way. These were people who did not even bother to brush away the flies that teemed on their largely unwashed bodies. This was a Place where the people had forgotten how to dream and where any aspiration, no matter how simple, was quickly dismissed, because everyone was sure that nothing would ever work.

Really, Ruby thought crossly. *Some people are their own worst enemies. There's something wrong with people who don't even bother washing or cleaning up after themselves. I hope it doesn't take me too long to walk though this Place because there is clearly nothing for me here.*

Don't be so quick to judge, my dear, the small, quiet voice that Ruby associated with her great-grandmother advised. *You don't know the full story, after all. There may well be a great deal more going on here than meets the eye.*

"Action is the antidote to despair."
Joan Baez

Ruby's shoes were fast wearing out and the few provisions that she had been able to take with her had almost been depleted. Despite her feeling that she would like to leave as soon as possible, she also knew that she had to find refuge somewhere soon. She was getting hungry and she was wise enough to know that there are times when it is better to ask for help than to struggle on, regardless of the consequences. *How I am going to find help here?* Ruby wondered. *These people look as though they don't have much more than me.*

It did not look like the sort of Place where anyone was likely to have either the inclination or the means to help and Ruby was very much afraid. Suddenly, she remembered a story that she had been told as a child, a story about the cannibals who lived in far-away lands. Ruby had never believed this story yet now, alone and in a Place that seemed to be filled with broken people, fear began to take a firm grip on her heart.

Don't worry, my dear, her great-grandmother's voice whispered softly to her. *If this is where you have come, this is where you are meant to be. Trust in yourself and you will be safe. You will see a sign, an entrance to a hidden world.*

Although nobody regarded her with any compassion or interest, Ruby continued to press on. Her great-grandmother had never let her down before. Surely this time would be no exception even if, as Ruby sometimes suspected, the voice she heard came from deep within herself. In truth, she added the words to the messages after feeling them.

Finally, Ruby saw a well-made door set into a carefully constructed stone wall. There was a heavy iron knocker on the door, rusty through lack of use. Could this be the entrance of which her great-grandmother's voice had spoken? Ruby knocked. Nobody came to the door, yet she thought she heard a faint rustle in the distance. She knocked again. Still, nobody came. At the same time, Ruby was pretty sure that she could hear some rather agitated muttering coming from behind the door. She knocked a third time and had the distinct impression that someone was watching her through a hole in the door. Still, nobody answered. Finally, just as she was about to leave, Ruby heard the rasp of metal on wood and looked up to see that a small grille in the door that she had not previously noticed had been opened. A pair of kindly eyes viewed her suspiciously from under a thick veil.

"Are you to marry God and dwell within?" the owner of the eyes said. "State your business and make it snappy. I don't have all day. There's a lot of work to be finished in here and it won't get done by itself!"

Ruby introduced herself. She explained that she had come from a distant Land and that she was in search of work, having exhausted her provisions. She held up one of her feet to expose her bleeding blisters and the holes in her shoes.

"I'm not looking for anything," Ruby said. "I just need a chance to work and rest for a while…"

"We don't take workers here," the woman told her. "This is a devotional community and we do all our own work for ourselves. In fact, we don't need any help with anything at all."

"I am very resourceful," Ruby said. "And I am also very tired, as I have come from very far away. I can work for food, and I won't disturb your devotions. I am not asking for charity. Please…"

As she spoke, Ruby felt her legs begin to give way underneath her. Just as she felt as though she were about to faint, the door opened and Ruby was hauled inside by two pairs of strong arms.

Looking around her in some surprise, Ruby found that she was in the company of two nuns, each of whom was dressed in a voluminous black habit and a wimple that covered their ears and hair, making them both look quite alike. They wore thick leather belts from which hung beads for praying and an array of gardening and building tools. Their hands were rough, as the hands of those used to hard physical labour.

The women looked at Ruby suspiciously, yet not unkindly.

"You had better come with us," one of them said after a few minutes. "You cannot stay long. We will take care of you and give you work to do for the time being. We can see that you are not from around here, so perhaps we can make some use of you. It would be a different matter if you were one of the locals; we won't have anything to do with them! It has been a very long time since we have had anything to do with anyone from the outside."

The Place where Ruby found herself was a convent, home to over fifty sisters. None of these women was younger than forty and it had been over twenty years since any of them had set foot outside the confines of their boundary walls. Unlike the people whom Ruby had seen in the countryside and villages outside the convent, all of the women looked very healthy and strong. They were well-dressed and nourished and seemed to be confident and assured. The reason for the stark contrast was soon clear, as the situation was explained to Ruby.

Twenty years earlier, the country in which the nuns lived had been rocked by a brief and savage civil war that had destroyed infrastructure and homes, ruined factories and farms, and reduced the population to abject misery. Teachers, doctors, nurses and most other professionals had all been killed, leaving a society that had already been very unequal without any of its natural leaders. This was a society that had never recovered from this onslaught on its integrity and now nobody seemed to be in charge of anything. Alcoholism was rife and most people just muddled through life rather badly and in a state of almost permanent confusion. Squabbles and spats were frequent and, with most people drunk most of the time, they often spiralled out of control, leaving grief and mayhem in their wake. This was a Place where all hope had been utterly destroyed and the past, when things had been better, had been relegated to mythology because few people in a Place where life expectancy had halved in one generation were old enough to clearly remember the way things used to be. This was a Place from which any aspiration for the future seemed to be banished and Ruby thought with a shudder of how terribly close she had come to not finding the convent and of how dangerous it would surely have been for her to be alone in the savage world beyond its walls.

Unaffected by the war that had raged outside their high stone walls, the nuns had decided to stay put and that is what they had done ever since. They had all entered the convent in hope of finding the spiritual and material purity that they yearned for and the closeness to their god that they craved. They had been terrified by the civil war that had, beyond their walls, destroyed so many of their family members and friends. When the fighting had finally come to nothing, as the unsanitary conditions had resulted in a plague that wiped out both commands without favouring one over the other, the nuns had ventured outside to see what they could do. They had been doubly horrified to see the depths of the depravity to which the remaining people, many of whom were traumatised former soldiers, had sunk. They were worse than animals as while animals do what they must, these people, it seemed, had chosen self-destruction and chaos.

Everyone was drinking, even many of the children. They had seen awful sights: a drunk mother, whose infant wailed piteously beside her and tried to reach her breast to suckle, men fighting in the street over scraps of bread, a dog beaten to death with a wooden bat, just for fun, and then left to fester in the hot sun. Shuddering, the women had all gone back inside their convent walls and sworn that they would never venture forth again. And they never had. Nor had any of the people outside ever tried to come in. It was as if the nuns had ceased to exist to the populace and their convent grounds become a sort of secret garden into which no man or woman dared set foot. In fact, superstitions and ghost stories had grown up, with wild claims and terrifying theories attached to the convent. Every child had been instructed, "Do what you are told or the nuns will get you!"

The reality was that the nuns had created a true parallel universe for themselves. Certainly, the nuns had created a little paradise that bore no resemblance to the gruesome scenes beyond the walls. The convent building was sturdy and well-built and it looked onto fields in which crops had been planted in orderly rows. Fish-ponds provided them with carp, trout and freshwater crayfish. Poultry laid fresh brown eggs and provided meat. Cows feasted on the lush green meadows of many mixed grass varieties that never needed either ploughing or fertiliser and freely gave their milk in exchange. All the animals offered manure in abundance, which went in turn to feed the fruit and vegetables and the bounty of food the nuns had planted. Honey-bees buzzed in and out of the flowers on the fruit-bushes that would presently be heavy with berries.

While all the nuns worked hard each and every day, they always had more than enough to eat (in fact, they frequently had to compost excess supplies) and they also found ample time to devote to prayer and reading. There were nuns who did the housework and cooked in the vast, cavernous kitchen, nuns who worked in the fields, and nuns who knew just which songs to sing to help the cows let down their milk. They practiced calligraphy, with specialised scribes who wrote the dictates by which they lived their lives in elaborate script. These dictates adorned the walls of the convent. They sang hymns in praise of their god and devoted entire evenings to reading and to discussing the finer details of some of the more esoteric scriptures. They devoted several hours a day to maintaining purity, in all its aspects. Frequent topics for discussion included how to avoid impure thoughts, what to do about the unpleasant smells that wafted in from across the high walls and how to maintain the blissful calm that reigned in their miniature universe. Nobody ever directly mentioned the world outside, as if by doing so they would threaten to import its chaos and confusion into their clean, tidy lives within.

The convent and its grounds were kept physically pure by maintaining an exceptionally high level of hygiene and cleanliness. The nuns had a fine tradition of medicine and healing and knew much about health, both physical and spiritual. The convent had become completely self-sufficient, even making its own lamps with wax from the convent hives, and there was never any need to interact with the people on the outside at all. In fact, to avoid worldly temptations and to maintain the purity of the convent complex, contact with the townspeople who lived outside the convent was completely prohibited. Ruby was the first outsider to have placed foot inside the convent walls for twenty years. She would never understand exactly why it was that they consented to let her enter in the first place. Perhaps it was that she was the only stranger to have visited in such a long time or perhaps they, like her, had had some sort of presentiment and knew that it was time for a fresh insight.

Seeing that Ruby had nowhere to go and feeling sorry for her plight, the nuns agreed to let her work in exchange for her keep and to set aside a few provisions every week until she had enough to leave with when it was time for her to move on. They inspected her worn, damaged shoes, and told her that they would send them to the convent cobbler for repair and that she would soon get them back as good as new. They gave her some of their home-spun clothes to wear and provided her with a simple, comfortable room in which to sleep. They could see that she was an industrious person, just like them, so they were happy to have her in the convent as a temporary guest - their first in many years. In their restrained way, they were actually quite excited about the whole thing and a bit curious about the world beyond as well, though they would never openly admit as much.

The nuns were kind and generous. In the spirit of maintaining purity in their convent, they asked Ruby precisely nothing about who she was and where she came from, in case anything in her answers might distract them from their raison d'être. There was only one rule by which she must abide: she must agree never to disturb them while they were at prayer. She could join them, if she wished, although this was not mandatory, otherwise she should stay away and keep quiet.

This seemed right and fair to Ruby, who happily agreed to work in their kitchen garden and do whatever she was told there. Her gardening skills were not very advanced and this would be an excellent opportunity to hone them. Knowing how to plant and grow things would always be useful in the future. Besides, she had been assured by the quiet voice of her great-grandmother that this was the right place for her to be and she felt confident that the reason for this would soon be revealed.

Ruby was set to work with a chubby, loquacious nun of about fifty-five called Sister Dorothy. Sister Dorothy observed the rules of silence during the prescribed hours and when she was allowed to speak, she spoke a lot, as if making up for the time lost to the silence she was forced to keep earlier. She talked of her long-ago childhood, when she had been a barefoot child in the village, before the days of the civil war. She talked about the battle that had raged beyond the convent and how frightened they had all been when they had looked over their walls and seen the bloodshed and destruction that had devastated the population of their village. She talked about their decision, twenty years earlier, to cease all contact with the outside world and how happy they had been ever since: "Now we no longer need to worry about anything. We take care of ourselves and we leave them to take care of themselves."

She spoke, briefly, about how they had had to bid farewell to friends and relatives on the outside, and how nobody knew whether these people were alive or dead and how it was more than probable that most of them had perished, if not during the Civil War and subsequent sickness, then in the lean, hungry years that had followed. For a moment, her voice faltered and Ruby thought that she could sense a moment of regret. Sister Dorothy quickly switched from this topic to that of the purity of the convent and how it was paramount that this purity be maintained, because it was only in this way that the nuns could ensure that their minds were elevated against worldly things and in a fit condition for communicating with their god.

Ruby thought about everything that Sister Dorothy had said as they had worked side-by-side in the convent garden. She liked a lot about the convent and its orderly way of life and she could quite understand how, in comparison to the wretched chaos that reigned outside, maintaining the status quo appealed to the community of women. Despite the many achievements of the inhabitants of the convent, something seemed to be wrong, something seemed to be missing. Although the nuns were clearly quite content with their lot and position in life, Ruby sensed that there was a problem that nobody was stating and that it might take someone from outside to recognise it and decide what to do about it before it grew to more troublesome proportions.

"There is something that has been puzzling me," she said to Sister Dorothy one day when they were both weeding around the lettuce. "The very youngest of the women here is forty. The average age must be about sixty-five. With no contact with the outside world, how will your convent continue to exist in the years to come? I have seen how some of the older nuns are beginning to find the work difficult and cumbersome. There are one or two who seem to be in their dotage. What will happen when they are so old that they need to be nursed? What will happen when even the youngest nuns have grown too old to grow their own food? Have you discussed it? Is there a plan?"

Sister Dorothy said nothing at all in response to these questions. It was as if Ruby had not spoken a word at all. Sister Dorothy started to work even more furiously than usual, turning over the soil with her trowel and inspecting the ground for pests, which she hacked viciously in two with her trowel when she found them.

"These horrid leatherjackets," Sister Dorothy said angrily. "They are capable of destroying an entire field of potatoes! The only thing you can do with them is root them out and destroy them! Destroy them, I say!"

Ruby realised that she had touched on a sore spot. This was the first time that she had seen Sister Dorothy stuck for words. For the time being, she retreated from the topic, thinking that she did not intend to stay away from it for long.

The next day, Ruby sat beside Sister Rose at dinner. Sister Rose was a great scholar who had raised the level of intellectual thought in the convent to such an extent that all the nuns could debate philosophy and scripture eloquently in several languages. After dinner in the evening, the nuns would often retreat to their living room for such a debate. Ruby was never able to follow what they were talking about, yet she did enjoy hearing their animated voices and watching their faces as they discussed and debated.

"I admire your work very much, Sister Rose," she said now, "and there is something that I would like to talk to you about. One thing troubles me when I listen to you, although I find you both wise and insightful. I have thought about it a lot and I just can't find any answers on my own. When the convent is no more, because no new people are allowed to set foot inside, what will happen to all your learning? When all the nuns are gone, there will be no literate people left in your country at all. Who will benefit then from all your books and the many years of work and wisdom that they represent? I hate to think of this beautiful convent and all its lands and buildings falling into disrepair because nobody knows how to maintain it. I hate to think of your manuscripts crumbling into dust because nobody is reading them or taking care of them."

Sister Rose said nothing. She changed the subject rather pointedly and avoided looking at Ruby for the rest of the meal. She poked her meal crossly with her fork and remarked that the stew could have done with a little more salt.

A little finger of doubt crept into Ruby's mind. She sighed. It was not always easy, knowing what to do. Perhaps she should just stop sticking her oar in? Look what had happened before, after all. She had started organising everyone and that had led to her expulsion from the only home that she had ever known. Yet, if nobody ever said anything, if nobody ever had any new ideas, things would never change. And surely that was not right. Surely not.

Don't give in, Ruby, her great-grandmother's voice counselled her. *Although you may not have all the answers, that does not matter, because you are asking the right questions and that is already a fantastic beginning.*

> *"Change is the constant, the signal for rebirth, the egg of the phoenix."*
> **Christina Baldwin**

In the middle of the convent complex, surrounded by fields and workshops, there was a chapel and above the chapel rose a belfry, tall and magnificent. An earlier generation of nuns had constructed it themselves from the stones that they plucked from the fields every year as they prepared them for planting. The belfry contained two great copper bells that were used to mark the time throughout the day and were rung by two of the burlier nuns, who pulled on thick ropes at regular intervals. Bells rang to announce time for prayer, for meal times, and for the ends and beginnings of work shifts. There was a rickety wooden ladder that had not been used for many years, which Ruby used now to mount the tower, taking care not to disturb the bats as they slept, their little heads tucked under their wings. The ladder was riddled with woodworm and Ruby marvelled at the fact that the nuns had allowed it to fall into such a state of disrepair, before realising that it must have been due to the fact that they never needed to mount the tower, because they had no interest whatsoever in seeing what was happening beyond the walls of the convent.

From the belfry, Ruby could see out across the land in which the convent was placed. Although the civil war had ended twenty years earlier, many buildings still lay in ruins. From her vantage-point, she could spot a school, a hospital and a fire station - all in pieces. The children of the land could be seen wandering aimlessly here and there, stepping over the comatose bodies of drunks who littered the landscape. It was not difficult to imagine how these same children were probably doomed to follow in the footsteps of the drunks over whose bodies they now stepped.

Ruby descended thoughtfully from the tower. Her thoughts and ideas about the convent were beginning to coalesce into a plan.

I think you know what you must do, her great-grandmother's voice whispered in her ear and Ruby nodded. She knew. Casting her doubts aside, she determined that she would do the right thing.

The very next day, Ruby approached the Mother Superior and asked her to grant her an audience.

"Mother Superior," she said. "If you will be so kind as to listen, I would like to tell you a story that I learned many years ago from my great-grandmother, when I was still just a little girl."

"Very well," said the older woman. "I like stories and I have about half an hour before I have to return to my duties. What is this story about?"

"I am going to tell you the story of Stone Soup." And with that, Ruby began to speak. Her voice began to work its magic and soon the Mother Superior was listening intently, almost as if Ruby had enchanted her.

***

Stone Soup

Once upon a time, in a Land not so very far from this one, there was a beautiful convent that had been built some generations earlier. It had fine buildings, beautiful lands and inhabitants who were gentle and hard-working, kind and wise. Yet this convent had no future and, despite all of its potential, it was obvious that it was just a matter of time before it simply ceased to exist. Around the convent there was a village and the people in the village had a great deal to offer their neighbours. Nonetheless, the two communities maintained themselves completely separately.

One day a wandering magician came to town and started to make soup with no more than a stone, a pot and some water. As he cooked in a quiet spot near the village green, an albino mouse ran up and down his sleeve. Hanging from the magician's waist was the rough figure of a man, fashioned from some dry grass. He looked mysterious indeed, yet also kind and friendly. Cautious, the townspeople did not disturb him, they just watched.

As the magician started to boil his stone, he invited the villagers to join in with whatever they had to offer, promising that when his Stone Soup was finished they would all share in the resulting feast. Little by little, the villagers added ingredients until the smell was so good that even the nuns were curious and poked their noses out from behind the heavy door of their citadel to see what was going on.

"Welcome," the magician said. "I had been wondering when you would turn up. Our soup is nearly done here and I think that all it needs to be just right is a vital ingredient or two that only you can offer…"

***

At this remark, the Mother Superior's lips pursed slightly. Ruby continued to talk, describing a wonderful village she knew where the community had come together to save a convent from extinction. She spun a vision of harmony and spoke of how the nuns in this village had often mistrusted the villagers, because they knew that some of them were thieves and liars and that others were unclean and lazy in their habits. Despite their concerns, in the end the nuns of Ruby's story had contributed so much to the village that the citizens came to care for them deeply and showed this affection in a myriad of ways that allowed both communities to grow together and move forward.

"I see," said the Mother Superior in leaden tones when Ruby had finished telling her story. "You are a very good storyteller although, if I may say so, you are not being very subtle. Tell me, how did this wonderful collaboration start?"

"Well," Ruby said. "In the beginning, the nuns made a public commitment to the village head man that they would give the villagers all their support in dealing with the social problems that had bedevilled them for years and the head man of the village actually helped train the new Mother Superior in ways of village management when the old Mother Superior suddenly passed before her time..."

"I am only seventy-two!" the Mother Superior remarked, rather sharply. "And I have never felt better or more vigorous than I do now!"

"Oh, I know," Ruby said. "I'm just telling a story. It is not about you. Not at all."

"Very well," said the Mother Superior, pursing her lips again.

Ruby suddenly noticed that the dining room in which they were speaking had gradually filled with women while she was speaking and that they were all listening intently to her. They had been so very quiet that she had not even noticed them come in. Now, raising her voice slightly so as to be heard better, Ruby continued to talk and to tell the magical story of a village that had been badly damaged by circumstances and that was just waiting for inspiration enough so they could save themselves.

Ruby's tale wove in many elements: how the local village fire station saved the convent in the village; how the children offered to climb the highest fruit trees so that they could throw the peaches and apricots into the nets below; how the nuns trained young girls and boys in how to teach, so that future generations would not grow up in the ignorance that had cursed the lives of their parents.

When Ruby had finished her tale to the Mother Superior, the whole dining room was silent and thoughtful. Of course, it did not take the nuns long to figure out that no such village had ever existed at all. That did not matter. The potent story of the village and the convent working together to build trust and cooperation where before none had existed was compelling to the nuns and started them thinking for the first time in many years about a subject that they had all been trying to avoid.

Finally Ruby broke the silence.

"I have had an idea," she said. "I understand that you wish to preserve the convent's purity and integrity, really I do. What I think, though, is that perhaps you could share some of all you know as a community by building a little outpost just outside the gates of the convent where some of the children can be taught a few basic skills. If they knew how to read and write, they might grow into men and women who are in a position to engage in commerce with people from other lands and if they knew how to produce food more effectively, there would be less hunger. The way things are now, it is hard to see how life can improve without some

67

outside help. In the village beyond your high convent walls, people are just too hungry to think about anything other than the next meal."

> *"Confidence imparts a wonderful*
> *inspiration to its possessor."*
> **John Milton**

The Mother Superior looked at Ruby, saying nothing. Her expression, however, seemed to be a little more open and a little less wary than it had been when Ruby had started telling the story.

"Besides," Ruby continued. "You never know. Perhaps some of those little girls will grow into young women who will want to join your community and continue your work."

Now the nuns looked at each other with new resolve. A few of them nodded their wimpled heads in recognition of the important truth that Ruby had just hit upon. Ruby had broached a subject that all of them thought about and that none of them dared mention – the future of the convent was at stake.

The nuns discussed Ruby's idea in great detail and, after several weeks of debate, they decided that it was worth trying, so long as there was the general understanding that if things did not go as they wished, they could retract back inside the convent whenever they wanted and return to their tried-and-tested ways of doing things. The unwelcome point that Ruby had made about the aging profile of the nuns in the convent had struck a very painful chord with them. This was something that everyone knew was a problem and yet nobody had ever had the courage to address it. Perhaps, finally, that time had come.

So it was, beneath the curious gaze of the townspeople, that the nuns built a simple structure just outside their back door and began to invite the first children in for their lessons.

Because the children were hungry and because many of them did not even know what a pencil and a piece of paper were, things did not go well at the beginning. In fact, they started off very badly. The little girls and boys were disruptive and lazy, insolent and rude. They seemed to have no interest in learning at all and, indeed, if the future of their country lay with them, things were even worse than the nuns had assumed.

Dismayed by this experience, the nuns began to consider retreating back inside the convent.

Ruby had another idea. "Perhaps," Ruby suggested to the nuns, "the children could all come inside for a hearty breakfast before starting work. Perhaps you could also teach them a little bit about growing food. I am sure it will be easier for them to study if they are not hungry. A lot of them really are awfully thin, aren't they? What is more, giving them breakfast would mean that you wouldn't have to compost your excess supplies anymore."

"Inside the convent? The townspeople have not been inside our convent for over twenty years! I don't think that it's going to work; not at all. Especially with such grubby little girls and boys! They would have to be washed first. Otherwise, just think of all the horrid germs that they might introduce."

"Well," Ruby said. "Perhaps they could do with a bit of a wash; that's really not such an insuperable obstacle, is it?"

For a week or two, the nuns debated Ruby's suggestion that the children should be given something to eat in the convent before starting their lessons and finally decided that her idea was acceptable. It was true that the children were very disruptive and that they were frequently difficult and even rude. It was also true that they could be sweet and it was painfully difficult to see how thin many of them were. So what if they were grubby and did not understand the convent's stringent hygiene rules? It was not their fault. They were just little children. They had not even been born when the civil war broke out and yet they were still its victims, all these years later, as much or even more than their parents were.

There was a large unused room in the convent and it was set up to be a refectory for the children. The nuns who laboured in the kitchen set about preparing simple, nourishing meals that would be easy for them to digest. Sister Dorothy herself took over the gardening lessons that gave the children a reprieve from their books and also taught them the rudiments of how to create food from a patch of earth and a packet of seeds. Once they had been fed, most of the children were hungry for much more than just the food that they were offered. They also craved the information, knowledge and skills that the nuns had decided to share with them.

After a while, some of the children's mothers approached the convent, quite shyly.

"Some of us used to know how to read and do sums," one of them said. "We were little children when the war broke out and we don't remember very well what it was like here before then. We had spent a couple of years in school and we had started reading and writing. I think we might get it back, with a little help. You know, there is nobody on the outside who is really able to give us what we need."

Sister Rose brought the women inside and over the months that followed, she helped them to remember all they used to know before the civil war had interrupted their education.

Goodness, Ruby's great-grandmother said quietly. *They have come a long way, haven't they? I think all the nuns needed was a little nudge in the right direction. It's lucky that you came along when you did, Ruby, my dear. And yet, doesn't it seem to you that there is something missing from this picture? All these voices are so high-pitched. I wonder what it could be...*

It is a long time since I even had a conversation with a man, Ruby thought. *I understand that the nuns wish to live in a woman-only community. All the same, it seems a little rough that the men should be the only ones left out in the cold. Wouldn't they benefit from knowing how to read and write too?*

Ruby had the feeling that this might be a difficult corner to fight. She took a deep breath and prepared to go into battle.

A little while later, some of the men of the town came and knocked on the door of the convent. When the Mother Superior answered it and, rather gruffly, asked the men what they wanted, they stood there with their hats held in their hands and addressed her respectfully with their eyes cast down. It was very clear that they were very much in awe of the older woman. They had had to gather their courage to come and address her, so whatever it was they needed was surely very important.

"We are strong," they said. "And we are willing to provide our labour if you can teach us how to farm properly, as well as giving reading lessons to our children. We remember our fathers working when we were small children, long ago before the civil war. They were all killed and there has never been anyone to teach us how to do anything. Most of us do our best. We know, though, that we are pretty rough around the edges."

The thought of letting men inside the convent walls was immensely distressing to the nuns, who discussed the dilemma for several weeks more. Could the men be trusted? Would the convent ever be the same again? And, most alarming of all, would they just barge in and start trying to tell the nuns what to do? Most of the nuns were getting on in years. However, they still remembered their bossy older brothers with considerable ambivalence. Finally, after consulting their holy scriptures and praying very earnestly for hours on end, they decided that giving the men the help that they requested was worth the risk, provided that a few basic rules were followed. After all it was not their fault that they were not women. Besides, men are usually very good for carrying heavy things about and as so many of the nuns were getting elderly and were not as strong as they had once been, this was something that might prove to be very useful indeed, provided it could be managed.

Ruby stayed at the convent for a year; the happiest year of her life since she had left her childhood behind her. That year was measured out in small ways - the regular chiming of the bells, the number of times that Ruby had to trim her nails and hair, as well as in larger ways. When Ruby finally realised that it was time for her to go, the convent had become a Place that resounded with the sounds of children laughing and children learning and where men carried heavy things about under the watchful eye of the nuns, while the women worked happily in the fields and pored over the books that they were now able to read.

The day before she left, Ruby climbed the chapel belfry and looked out at the town that had horrified her so deeply the first time she had seen it, just twelve short months before. While it was still a poor, dusty sort of a Place, there were no longer hordes of children in dirty clothes, wandering here and there. There were still some comatose drunks, to be sure. Now, however, Ruby could see that they were much less numerous and that even the ones who did still regularly pass out on the dusty streets generally scooped themselves up and shuffled home at the end of the day. The school, hospital and fire station were half-built and already manned by nuns, bustling here and there and teaching the townspeople all they knew. Ruby felt confident that this was now a Place with a bright future.

Ruby felt restless and suspected that there was very little left here for her to do. Everything seemed to be working perfectly and she had no advice to give. Nor, she felt, was there anything more for her to learn here. So, happy as she had been in this place of hard work and prayer, she wondered if it was not time to leave.

Great-grandmother, she asked. *Tell me, is it time for me to go?*

A voice came back to her, soft and gentle: *Yes, my darling. The people here know how to make Stone Soup now, you should continue with your journey.*

> *"The best way to predict*
> *the future is to invent it."*
> **Alan Kay**

Lessons from A Village Behind Closed Doors

The attacks on New York on September 11th, 2001 are often referred to as a watershed - the end of one era and the beginning of another. We all remember where we were and what we were doing when the attacks occurred and the political and military decisions taken in their wake continue to impact on our world, as they surely will for quite some time to come. I happened to be in New York on business when the World Trade Centre was attacked. At that time, I was working hard to close a deal that I was quite excited about. I was also excited to be in New York, a city that I love and that I regard as the epitome of the modern world; yet as soon as the planes hit the towers, my worldview shifted. Suddenly, for me, New York was no longer a safe, wonderful, exciting place, it had become an awful trap from which I needed to escape as quickly as possible. I experienced all the symptoms of profound anxiety that many suffered that day and knew that I would not be able to relax until I left the city.

What I was reacting to was not merely the events themselves, dreadful as they were. I was also reacting to my perception of the events. I was affected more by the reactions of the people around me than by what was going on in my own world. Before I could react appropriately, I had to stop and really look around. I realised that, in order to become effective again, I had to accept my situation. In New York, I reconnected with friends and colleagues and we got back to work, during which time I provided support to anyone I encountered

74

who needed it. We decided that if we put our lives on hold, we were letting the terrorists win.

While our perceptions of events, people and places can be useful, they never provide the full picture. Perceived danger is just that - perceived. It can take over if we let it, as in the example of the secluded nuns in Ruby's story. In order to make rational, appropriate decisions about the place or situation we find ourselves in, it is necessary to acquire the ability to incorporate our instinctive perceptions into a more complete understanding, rather than relying on them alone, which means recognising that you are being affected by what is going on. In order to see most clearly, you need to stop to take a breath and really listen to your surroundings with a calm presence. It is an oft used excuse to claim that when we are at the mercy of circumstances, we somehow have permission to be stuck in them. This is not the case. I have seen others, as well as myself, be able to transcend circumstances and even terror by taking the time to be more fully aware.

Understanding how perception affects your view of reality can greatly assist you when applied towards challenging people or situations. I have often observed that, by embracing that which you have fought hard against, you can increase your chances of winning. Just as a judo master will use their opponent's own momentum to toss them lightly onto the mat, unexpectedly moving towards the point of view you have been trying to avoid can yield great benefits. It's as if opposing sides create an obstacle between them that embodies the impasse. When one side stops playing this game, the other is sometimes left to ponder the strangeness of maintaining a barrier alone. In past professional situations, I have handed in my signed resignation, not because I wanted to resign nor as any kind of protest. I did it to give the person in charge the confidence that I was working at their pleasure and not my own and that they could accept the document, or not, at any time of their choosing. The result was that any tension that had crept in between us was dissipated and I was able to get on and do what needed to be done. While I do not suggest this as a common course of action, it was surprisingly freeing and effective and the resignation in question was torn up before the ink had fully dried. By changing the overarching perceptions that were present at those times, I was able to create a more productive environment.

A RECIPE FOR STONE SOUP

One generous portion of belief

One or more enthusiastic catalysts

One well defined context, communicated well

Testing for bad eggs so that you can leave them out

A heaping spoonful of emotion and trust

The ability to react proportionately and
level-headedly in times of crisis or change

In 1966, the philosopher Kenneth Burke published a volume called *Language as Symbolic Action*, which included an essay entitled *Definition of Man* (subsequently republished as *Definition of Human*). This essay included the ground-breaking concept of the terministic screen. Burke defined humankind as follows: "Man is the symbol-using inventor of the negative separated from his natural condition by instruments of his own making goaded by the spirit of hierarchy and rotten with perfection."[2] In other words, the one thing that distinguishes us from all the other animals is our ability to assign symbols to things. This is the essence of language and of abstract thought. All the actions that we take as human beings are rich in symbols. These serve not just to explain to ourselves who we are and where we belong, they also help us to define the world. Burke points out, as an example, how the titles that we give to ourselves and to others describe our role in society, terms such as "working class" and "aristocratic" or "housewife" and "provider."

Burke coined the phrase "terministic screens" to discuss the ramifications of our choice of certain terms over others in the names we give to the things and people in our world, saying, "Even if any given terminology is a reflection of reality, by its very nature as a terminology it must be a selection of reality and to this extent it must function also as a deflection of reality."[3] In other words, the terms that we choose to describe things are very revealing and predispose us to think and feel about things in a certain way. By listening to the different terms and expressions people use to form their different perspectives, we often gain a more effective view of reality than if we rely on our own single perceptions and descriptions. Ask at least three other unrelated people about something and you will nearly always gain insight beyond your own into the perceived reality.

---

[2] Burke, 1966, 16.

[3] Burke, 1966, 45.

<u>A RECIPE FOR STONE SOUP</u>

One generous portion of belief

One or more enthusiastic catalysts

One well defined context, communicated well

Testing for bad eggs so that you can leave them out

A heaping spoonful of emotion and trust

The ability to react proportionately and
level-headedly in times of crisis or change

A triple dose of reality

In his book, *Community[4]*, Peter Block publishes a rare insight direct from Werner Earhart, and this rather difficult to follow example has lead me to my view of the holistic present. What follows is a portion of that letter.

"I suggest you make it clear that the future that one lives into that shapes one's being and action in the present...the reason that it appears that it is the past that shapes one's being and action in the present is that for most people the past lives in (shapes) their view of the future.

"...it is only by completing the past (being complete with the past) such that it no longer shapes one's being and action in the present that there is room to create a new future (one not shaped by the past – a future that wasn't going to happen anyhow). Futures not shaped by the past (i.e., a future that wasn't going to happen anyhow) are constituted in language.

"In summary, (1) one gets complete with the past, which takes it out of the future (being complete with the past is not to forget the past); (2) in the room that is now available in the future when one's being and action are no longer shaped by the past, one creates a future (a future that moves, touches and inspires one); (3) that future starts to shape one's being and actions in the present so that they are consistent with realizing that future."

---

[4] Block, 2008, p. 16.

As Ruby noted about the fate of the enclosed world that the nuns had created for themselves, societies or human organisations of any size that will not embrace change are doomed to atrophy. History has given us innumerable examples of this simple truth. Consider the fate of the inhabitants of Easter Island, discussed by Jared Diamond in *How Societies Choose to Fail or Succeed*. The people that formed the small island community devoted a huge amount of effort to creating the spectacular megalithic heads that attract so many tourists today, while basing their economy on the tree coverage of their island. When the last tree had been cut down, the society was no more. I sometimes fear the same will happen on a catastrophically wider scale as humanity cuts down the last trees on our island Earth.

In *The Time Paradox*, Zimbardo and Boyd discuss how our attitudes toward time influence every aspect of our lives. They explore how people spend their time and how attitudes towards time impact on one's likelihood of achieving happiness and success. Specifically, they look at whether people are future-oriented or present-oriented. In today's world, many people are future-oriented, always focussing on what they need to do "now" to make things better "then." Some people feel that it is worth learning how to be present-oriented, so as to enjoy life as it happens, even if this means working less and investing less in the future. The authors suggest that the best approach is to find a healthy balance between focussing on the present and focusing on the future.

An excessive focus on the "now" can be bad for relationships and bad for business, as it can lead to a desire for instant gratification. Zimbardo and Boyd cite some of the recent financial scandals in the United

States as an example of how an excessive focus on the present can be bad for business. A balanced approach is one where the past is interpreted generally favourably, where the present is enjoyed and there is a focus, yet not an excessive focus, on the future. Time-balanced people do not ponder unhappy periods in the past. The Dalai Lama refers to this balance as the "holistic present," which contains both past and future considerations, bringing value to those who are living in it. The past brings access to wisdom and the future frames, and gives greater purpose to being in the now, while the attention is on the present moment. The central message is that the present moment should be approached with a warmth of spirit in order to live with a more holistic perception in a holistic present.

A RECIPE FOR STONE SOUP

One generous portion of belief

One or more enthusiastic catalysts

One well defined context, communicated well

Testing for bad eggs so that you can leave them out

A heaping spoonful of emotion and trust

The ability to react proportionately and
level-headedly in times of crisis or change

A triple dose of reality

A preheated holistic present

A person's individual past is like a foreign country in that it is often seen more clearly through the eyes of a guide. When attempting to gain perspective on past troubles, it can be helpful to converse with others, as the solution does not usually lie on the road on which you travel back and forth, rather it is off the road, often at right angles, and in the eyes of others that you can truly see what is holding you back. In judging ourselves, we are often our own worst enemies.

I know many people who have issues with money and come at the world from a position of scarcity that informs how they interpret it. In their eyes, this is simply how it is. When someone comes to inspire them, they simply ignore it. Yet if they really get into honest conversation with someone else with a different perspective, someone who is also patient enough to listen, they can start to see a different perspective and, from this different perspective, their own illogical ideas can suddenly be seen for what they are. I have had the privilege of reversing many people's scarcity view of the world and turning it into a view of abundance simply by getting people to see a different vision for the future; one that is not rooted in their past or in their past-informed view of the future as Ruby was eventually able to do with the nuns.

A RECIPE FOR STONE SOUP

One generous portion of belief

One or more enthusiastic catalysts

One well defined context, communicated well

Testing for bad eggs so that you can leave them out

A heaping spoonful of emotion and trust

The ability to react proportionately and
level-headedly in times of crisis or change

A triple dose of reality

A preheated holistic present

A substantial dollop of perspective

It pays to be widely read, interested in many things and aware of many current issues so that you can genuinely have something in common with almost anyone. Since spending time in Ireland, I have learned that the Irish are particularly good at a very characteristic form of networking. When you first meet someone from Ireland, they usually start by quizzing you about where you are from.

"You're from Australia!" they declare in delight. "My best friend from school lives in Australia! He has a house in Sydney. I have never been there myself. I haven't seen him for ten years. Are you from Sydney?"

"Oh no, I'm from Melbourne," you answer. "I don't actually know Sydney that well." You try to change the subject to something more relevant. Nothing works. They are like a dog with a bone; there's no way they are going to give it up.

"Melbourne!" they cry with the air of someone who has struck the jackpot. "And that's where his wife is from! She is Melbourne born and raised. Amazing! What part of Melbourne did you grow up in?"

"Camberwell," you say. You don't really know the point of this. Melbourne is a very big city. The chances of you knowing his friend or his friend's wife are really very small.

"Camberwell. Is that near the Docklands?"

"It is not that far. Actually, we used to go there for a walk most weekends." You have become resigned to following this conversation through to the end, although you really don't see where it is going.

"No way! My friend's wife always says she loves the Docklands. They go there every time they are in Melbourne. Sure, you've probably walked past each other and never knew it. What a small world!"

This is a very simple and effective way of forging a connection. Suddenly, a feeling of closeness exists where none had been before. This relatedness comes out of nothing and yet it has some power and can grow deeper over time. By now, you've built a relationship, tenuous as it may seem, and information has been exchanged. When I first came to Ireland, I found this ritual very odd. Now, I find it indispensable and, in fact, it is almost always possible to find a connection with someone. I now know the ritual for what it is - an invitation to friendship.

One of the best things you can do for people is to find out what they really are interested in and what they need and then introduce them to a person or a book that can assist them with what they are doing. To be able to do this effectively, you must be both widely read and widely networked and this takes a solid investment in time. Fortunately, with the Internet and even a small thirst for knowledge, the research portion of this time investment is a lot easier than it used to be and a lot more fun. In such conversations it is also important to keep your principles in mind. Before starting any conversation, I always try to ask myself, "What can I provide this person that will make their day?" When I do not remember to ask this question, the conversations are never as good or productive as when I do.

A RECIPE FOR STONE SOUP

One generous portion of belief

One or more enthusiastic catalysts

One well defined context, communicated well

Testing for bad eggs so that you can leave them out

A heaping spoonful of emotion and trust

The ability to react proportionately and
level-headedly in times of crisis or change

A triple dose of reality

A preheated holistic present

A substantial dollop of perspective

A variety of questions including
self-questioning without self-doubt

According to Allan and Barbara Pease in their books about human relationships[5], there is a body of research that shows that women's brains, generally speaking, dedicate much more space to speech than men's. This means that, on average, women tend to be better at multitasking and can pick up on a much wider range of human emotion than their male counterparts. This would seem to make women naturally better able to be cat herders, or catalysts, as the ability to keep track of multiple things at once and to better understand emotions and subtle emotional signals from other people are vital traits of both. I suspect that, in days gone by, when most top leaders had "a very powerful personal private secretary," there was probably a lot of catalysing on the leader's behalf. We have all heard the saying that behind every great man there is a great woman. In the past, the achievements of too many of

---

[5] Pease and Pease, 2001, 2006.

these great women remained unsung. Now, things are beginning to change and, in more countries around the world, women are being heard more than ever. While we could still do with many more women leaders at every level of society, both male and female leaders alike will benefit enormously from being able to tap into their own reserves of female energy.

Along with feminine sensitivity, leaders of both sexes also need gravitas. Our society is still waiting for enough women to be empowered to assume necessary gravitas in the workplace. Gravitas is a two way street; it must be assumed by the catalyst and, at the same time, granted by the audience, and its success will depend much on contact. It is difficult for people to grant gravitas to people outside of their normal context. Consider how much you grant to a doctor when you go and see her in her office and find her in a white coat and stethoscope. You may well be quite willing to literally put your life in the hands of a complete stranger in that context. Yet, witness the same doctor on the drilling deck of an oil rig giving technical instructions to a gang of burly seasoned men who have been working on the same oil rig for years. I see new people come into organisations all the time, trying to impress everyone without first getting into the context of the situation at hand. If our oil rig doctor had spent a season proving to the guys that she knew her stuff, things might be different. What I want for my own daughter is for her to be able to look anyone in the eye and immediately command respect for who she is, yet although we have made great strides towards equality in the world, in order for this to happen we still have a lot of changes to make on both sides.

A RECIPE FOR STONE SOUP

One generous portion of belief

One or more enthusiastic catalysts

One well defined context, communicated well

Testing for bad eggs so that you can leave them out

A heaping spoonful of emotion and trust

The ability to react proportionately and
level-headedly in times of crisis or change

A triple dose of reality

A preheated holistic present

A substantial dollop of perspective

A variety of questions including
self-questioning without self-doubt

Several spoonfuls of leadership
gravitas steeped in female energy

If the longest journey begins with a single step, it can be said that the biggest movements start with a single phrase - often "I am" or "We are." When something big needs to be done, a balance must be struck between seeing the big picture of what has to be achieved and knowing what macro constraints and micro level activities need to be undertaken to reach the larger goal. Both of these sides must be communicated clearly so that each person in the team has a map of where they are going and, at the same time, is motivated to take those single steps.

An important skill for a catalyst is the ability to be able to zoom in and out of a problem, going down to a great level of detail, while being able to pull back quickly to see and share the big picture, to allow for effective communication at all times. Often, the catalyst's job is to be the interpreter of the wishes of the leadership, able to grasp the big picture and to translate that picture into the detailed and prosaic action to be carried out by both individuals and specialists. This balance must be carefully maintained, as it is easy for the catalyst to become bogged down in minutiae and micro management, causing productivity to cease and disempowering individuals in the team.

Delegation is a fine tool, and inspiration a far better one. A catalyst's job should be to make things happen using existing chains of command without being forced into the position of actually delivering each piece themselves, as Ruby was able to do through her stories and suggestions. The greatest inspiration comes from listening and, counter-intuitively, it is often most inspiring when leaders listen to those who follow them. Here, the catalyst can also play a role in making sure nothing is missed. I actually believe that, with the right questions and attentive listening, one can inspire anyone to do almost anything. Listening, of course, is also about knowing when and how to introduce questions that will not lead, but, will help the person who is talking to reveal what they really think.

If you want to succeed at being a catalyst you do need to ask questions, yet instead of providing the answer, you need to really listen to hear the answers because if you assume, as Benny Hill once illustrated to great comic effect, you make an "ass" out of "u" and "me." This is a tricky balance, though, as the person asking the questions is the one in control of the conversation and people often quickly resent not being in control. The phrase "I'll ask the questions here" is synonymous in the movies with tough cops and evil villains, all of whom have their victim at their mercy. This means that you also need to be able to listen out for what people want by listening attentively to the questions they ask you. Often, people use indirect speech as a way of telling you what they really want, asking questions about one subject to try and gauge your feelings on another. In order to determine their true interests, you have to be prepared to listen carefully to what they are saying and you can do this by listening actively. Active listening includes nodding and responding non-verbally to what they say and listening with your eyes as well as your ears. Observe their hands, their posture, and the cadence and speed and inflection of their words and, once you have listened, test your understanding. No one will complain if you ask questions to test whether you have gotten the message right and people are often relieved if you pick up on what they were trying to say and especially how they feel about something without them having to come right out and say it. While you may not know the answers, through active listening you can possess the tools needed to find them.

<u>A RECIPE FOR STONE SOUP</u>

One generous portion of belief

One or more enthusiastic catalysts

One well defined context, communicated well

Testing for bad eggs so that you can leave them out

A heaping spoonful of emotion and trust

The ability to react proportionately and
level-headedly in times of crisis or change

A triple dose of reality

A preheated holistic present

A substantial dollop of perspective

A variety of questions including
self-questioning without self-doubt

Several spoonfuls of leadership
gravitas steeped in female energy

A large measure of inspiration fortified by deep listening

A Village Behind Closed Doors

CHAPTER FOUR

Wheels Within Wheels

*"Chaos is the score upon
which reality is written."*
Henry Miller

That night, Ruby packed up her provisions and, as soon as the sun began to appear over the horizon, she went away. She knew that she would be missed. She also knew that she would not be missed for long, as this was now a Place full of friendship and creativity. Ruby did not know where her travels would take her next, yet she trusted her great-grandmother's advice, as it had never steered her in the wrong direction before. Wherever she was led, she was willing to go.

Ruby walked for a long way to the south, until she reached a highway that skirted the boundaries of the long-neglected country that was finally beginning to blossom again. The highway stretched out, long and flat, in front of her. A dusty carriage, rickety and slow on solid wooden wheels, came trundling down the highway and stopped in front of Ruby. There were a number of people seated in the carriage, all of them covered in heavy dust from head to foot. They wiped their faces with the napkins that they had brought for the purpose and smiled at Ruby, who realised that she was meant to travel with them, for reasons that she did not yet know.

"Are you going to the City?" the driver asked. "That's where we are heading. We won't be fast, yet we'll surely get there a lot more quickly than you will on foot."

Ruby thought for a moment. She had left the convent without a plan as to where to go, secure in the knowledge that she would find a sign that would provide her with the insight she needed. Was this that sign? She waited for her great-grandmother's voice.

Yes, she heard, as though from very, very far away.

"Yes, I think I am," she said and climbed on board for the first carriage ride of a long and often uncomfortable journey.

As she travelled Ruby tried to get to know each of her drivers as well as possible. Because it was a long trip, two men took turns to steer the carriage. The carriage was of the old-fashioned clockwork variety, which required them to stop every so often to have the contraption wound up, a procedure that took some fifteen minutes, took considerable strength and provided ample opportunity for the passengers to chat or wander discreetly behind roadside bushes to take care of personal matters. . Because the journey was long and slow, people were pleased to have someone on board to entertain them and Ruby quickly made several friends. They were surprised by the earnest girl who told stories with the air of a true raconteuse and could also listen attentively for hours. They had never met anyone quite like her and she certainly gave them plenty to think about.

As Ruby travelled into another new Land, she looked around herself in fascination. There was much to see. Among the things that enthralled Ruby the most were the carriages that filled the roads or that, frequently, sat at the side of the road while the drivers attended to a broken wheel axle, wound up the clockwork mechanism that drove the contraption or fixed other problems. They were all quite disorganised and Ruby often heard the drivers lament that they could not find a way to cooperate with each other as everyone seemed to want to do his own thing. Also, each carriage maker had a different type of mechanism so spare parts were not easy to come by and it was unlikely that anyone who passed by was going to be in a position to help. There was not even consensus about which side of the road to use, with the result that everyone had to move very, very slowly so as to minimise the damage resulting from the inevitable accidents.

Ruby puzzled over this situation as she made her way closer and closer to the City. Surely there must be a better system! How much closer together all these countries would be if only there were an effective way to move between them. Ruby thought about her first journey on foot, when she had been banished from her Land and forced to walk the long distance to the convent; a trip that had been both uncomfortable and dangerous. How much easier that journey would have been if there had been another system. And yet what could work better? Ruby did not know. Although she had been banished from her home a year before, she still had not travelled very widely and there was much she did not understand. Perhaps her destination would provide her with some opportunities to learn. She certainly hoped so.

Finally, they arrived at the carriage station on the outskirts of the City. Another surprise awaited Ruby when she was asked to pay a considerable fee in return for the trip and she ended up handing over more than half her provisions.

"I'm sorry," the driver said apologetically as he packed Ruby's provisions carefully into his burlap sack. "I know the price is high. The thing is that my overheads are very high too, with the constant maintenance and the repairs I have to carry out every time I bump into someone else. That's the problem. Believe me, I would not ask you to hand over so much if I didn't have to."

"I quite understand," Ruby said politely. And she did. She had experienced for herself what a tortuous business it was, getting traffic to go anywhere. Ruby was thoughtful as she walked away. Surely there must be a better way to go about doing things than this.

The City was a wonderful place, the best and worst of all worlds seemed to blend here, creating a heady mix of people, sights, smells and sounds that was quite unlike anything Ruby had ever experienced before and that almost overwhelmed her with sensation. Why had nobody ever told her about the City before? Ruby had had no idea that it was even possible for so many people to live crammed into the same space. She felt dizzy, just thinking about the possibilities that the City engendered. This was something utterly new. Something that she had never even contemplated before.

Everywhere Ruby looked, there were great, tall buildings that seemed to reach the sky, so high did they soar. Birds whirled and soared high in the air and yet they were still very far below the upper storeys of those mighty buildings, so high did those majestic edifices reach. Ruby had never seen such impressive buildings in her life. Even the magnificent Palace that had been built for the Bureaucrat-in-Chief in her home country had not been the match of these marvellous structures. The streets below were busy with adults going to work, mothers with babies, old people shopping and children walking their dogs or going to school. In a single street, Ruby thought with wonder, there were probably more people than lived and worked in the entire convent she had just left behind. What an extraordinary level of organisation must be required just to stop the whole thing from descending into chaos!

Not everything was organised, Ruby quickly realised. In fact, a significant degree of disorganisation was in evidence all around her. In the City most people walked, some of them carrying considerable burdens with them. Lumbering carriages could also be seen, bringing goods and people to a range of destinations at a speed barely superior to that of the pedestrians. The drivers all looked extremely harried and with good reason, as the carriages had to stop constantly to be wound up or negotiate a way through the traffic without hurting anyone. This was all a considerable challenge and rude, yet understandable, blasphemies could be heard being uttered loudly on all sides. Driving one of those heavy carriages did not look like a job that anyone in their right mind would want to do and, in fact, more than a few of the drivers had rather alarming gleams in their eyes, as though they had already had enough, several years before. The passengers, for their part, were all covered in dust and utterly exhausted from the long and stressful journeys that they had just undertaken. Ruby already knew that public transport was an enormously costly business, and that must be why so many of the pedestrians struggled under huge burdens, she reasoned, rather than paying to be driven in a carriage.

Ruby had just a few provisions left, and she knew very well that they would not last forever, so when she saw a faded sign in the window of a factory announcing a vacancy, she went straight in to look for work.

Above the gate, a gilded scroll proudly announced: "Making the finest carriages for the best people for over two hundred years!" The gate was an impressive structure that spoke of a long-established company that took great pride in its work and in its history. Only at a second glance did one notice that the gilt paint was peeling rather badly around the edges and that the sign seemed to have seen better days.

Ruby hesitated for a moment. Was this factory really a place where she wanted to go? It looked a little too grand for her, she thought, despite the peeling paint. After all, she was just a girl from a small land far away. What did she know about living and working in the big City? What did she know about big factories?

Nothing, Ruby told herself glumly. *You don't know anything about this sort of thing. Perhaps you should have stayed away.*

I think you should go in, her grandmother's voice counselled her gently. *You didn't find yourself here without a reason. Remember: there is a purpose for everything and within yourself you have the power to deal with whatever comes up.*

So Ruby did step through the gilded gate, albeit rather hesitantly, as if someone was likely to chastise her for daring to step forward.

Inside, it was clear that things were not going so well for this particular business, as many of the windows overlooking the factory courtyard had been repaired with brown-paper and packing-tape, and walls and doors were festooned with peeling paint. A leak in the middle of the courtyard had been left unrepaired and a couple of scruffy pigeons were taking a bath in the muddy water that had pooled where the cobblestones dipped in the middle. There were sounds of activity coming from several buildings, so she could tell that something was going on. At the same time, the kiosk just inside the gate looked as though it must have been empty for several years.

Ruby made her way to the central office, where she was greeted by a white-haired receptionist who glanced at her in evident astonishment that anyone should have responded to the flyblown notice on the gate.

"What on earth do you want?" the receptionist asked. "We don't generally get people walking in from off the street around here. And you don't even look as though you are from around here, if you don't mind me making the observation. Why, you look just about as uncomfortable as a fish out of water!"

Ruby unloaded her pack of provisions and placed it on the floor. Her arms ached. She was glad to put it down. Depleted as it was after having paid the carriage driver with half of her precious provisions, she was exhausted and its weight had become very burdensome.

"I have come about the job," Ruby said. "Do you mind if I leave my pack here for a little while? I have been walking for quite a long time and it is beginning to feel rather heavy."

The receptionist smiled at Ruby, a trifle uncertainly, and ushered her into a waiting room where four empty chairs leaned disconsolately against the wall.

"I'll tell the Boss that you are here for an interview," the old woman said rather nervously. "We've had the sign up for weeks and nobody has come because everybody knows...well, never mind. Anyway, he will probably see you now. He doesn't really have anything else to do, anyway."

Indicating to Ruby where she should sit and wait, the older woman disappeared into a back room. Five minutes later, she returned: "He will see you now. Good luck, my dear!"

When Ruby entered the Boss's office, she found herself in a dark, oak-lined room with little natural light. On the other side of a heavy mahogany desk sat a man with his back to her looking out a window onto what must have been a factory floor at a time when the factory had been more productive than it was now. Through the dusty glass Ruby could see work areas that were evidently neglected, with piles of cut-off pieces of wood tossed here and there, cobwebs lining the legs of the work tables and several broken windows badly patched together with cardboard and tape.

"Come in and close the door," the Boss said, still with his back turned to her. "And sit down on the chair beside the desk."

Ruby sat down and waited for the Boss to turn around. After several more minutes of gazing intently, he did. Ruby sat forward in her uncomfortable chair and held out her hand for him to shake. He just looked at her, very coldly, and after a moment she withdrew her hand again with a little shiver. Ruby had had to deal with many challenges during her short lifetime. She had had to face distrust and dislike and even hatred. There had been times when it had seemed to her that she was simply facing one difficult challenge after another. While this had always been stressful, there had rarely been times when she had not soon found an answer and an approach to take. Rank indifference, though, was something new and she did not like it. Even the Bureaucrat-in-Chief had had the good grace to look hassled by her presence, when he had issued the decree of exile and sent her away. At least then she had known that she was not simply being ignored.

"Well," the man said while shuffling through a little pile of papers on his desk. "What makes you want to work here? And make it snappy; I have got a lot to do and I'm sure that neither of us wants to waste time."

"I'm from far away," Ruby said, "I have just found myself in your City. I have some provisions and I know that they won't last forever, so I'm looking for work. I saw the sign in your window and I thought..."

"A slip of a thing like you!" the Boss said scornfully. "What do you know about work? You look as though the wind might blow you away. And shouldn't you be in school?"

Ruby was taken aback by the man's unpleasant tone and dismissive words and she had half a mind to leave straight away. Still, she reminded herself that she needed the work and that she knew nobody in this unfamiliar city and swallowed her words.

"I am not at all afraid of hard work," Ruby said in an even tone. "And if you let me work here, you'll soon see for yourself. If you hire me, you won't regret it." "And," she added, "if you actually looked at me, you would see that I am a grown woman and that I cannot have been in school for several years now."

Finally prompted by her words, the Boss looked at Ruby from beneath his heavily furrowed brows and flicked a mangled paperclip scornfully in her general direction. It was all Ruby could manage not to walk away in outrage. She reminded herself that she was not in a position to be choosy, especially as she had had to pay the carriage driver with almost half of her provisions and only had enough to see her to the end of the week. It was quite intimidating being all alone in the City for the very first time and Ruby knew that she had to find a way to take care of herself very quickly.

> *"Courage is doing what you're afraid to do. There can be no courage unless you're scared."*
> **Eddie Rickenbacker**

"Very well," the angry man said with the air of someone granting a great favour. "I will give you a chance. You can start work in the polishing department. It's hard to see how you could do any damage there. I warn you though, people often don't last long here. They cannot take the pressure. This is a place where people have to work long, hard hours and I am sure that you are not used to that sort of thing."

"Indeed," Ruby said politely, although inwardly she was seething. "Thank you very much."

What a rude man, Ruby thought as she left the room. *I wonder why he is so cross?* She had been surprised to note, when he got up from behind the desk to show her out of the room, that the man was much younger than she had originally thought, probably about her own age and certainly not more than a year or two older. This seemed to make his crossness all the more surprising. How could life have already made him so jaded and annoyed? Ruby had certainly had some ups and downs in her life and she never let herself get as cross as this.

I think that this man is very important for you, Ruby's great-grandmother observed sagely. *I think that he will play a very important role in your life.*

Nonsense, thought Ruby. *This is the most unpleasant person I have ever met. As soon as I can, I will find work somewhere else.*

The polishing room was a hive of activity when Ruby was brought in to start work the next morning. She was still very tired after a night with little sleep. She had found temporary lodgings in a ramshackle boarding-house near the fruit-and-vegetable market downtown and, with everything so strange and new, had found it hard to rest. Additionally, the vendors had started putting together the stalls at five o'clock in the morning, a business that seemed to entail an atrocious amount of clanging and banging, and quite a surprising amount of vigorous and livid cursing. Ruby had tried to hide her head under her pillow and quickly found that that did not help. Unused to the clamour of the City, she had found it impossible to get back to sleep. It was a painfully difficult night for Ruby as she tossed and turned. She found herself wishing that she could turn back time and be once more at home in her Land, where everything seemed familiar and safe, especially with the rosy glow of hindsight. She found herself thinking about how much easier life would have been if she had just stayed quiet and put up with the Bureaucrat-in-Chief's absurd rulings. Then, just as the sun appeared over the horizon and heralded the day, she reminded herself of all the success and growth that she had seen at the convent and resolved to face the next day and whatever came after it with all the courage that she could muster.

Despite her exhaustion, Ruby was determined to make a good impression in her new job and prove that nasty Boss wrong about her. Who did he think he was, telling her that she did not know anything about work?

The first thing that Ruby noticed when the Boss introduced her to the other workers in the polishing room, was that none of them looked her in the eye or so much as raised their heads to look at the Boss. The second thing she noticed was that the Boss had not bothered to remember her name or even to write it down so as to have a note to refer to. Ruby was glad when he left and she took her place to await her instructions at the long table where the workers sat.

The foreman of the polishing room was a thin, grey-haired man called Matthew, whom the boss had introduced as having been at the company since he left school. Ruby could see that this must have been quite a while ago. Matthew looked as if he lived and slept in the factory, and he seemed to be a loyal and hard worker. Matthew explained to Ruby how her job was to be done. As the woodworkers finished with each piece of finely worked wood, it was brought to the polishing room to be individually polished, first with coarse sandpaper, then with fine sandpaper and finally with kid leather soaked in linseed oil. Then, all the pieces were taken to the assembly room where they were put together by the master assemblers, following which the entire carriage was returned to the polishers, who did their work all over again, this time on the complete piece.

"Goodness," said Ruby. "I had no idea that polishing a carriage was such a complicated procedure."

"It certainly is," Matthew agreed. "I am the third generation of my family to work right here, in the polishing room and even I am still learning how to perfect my tasks. That, my dear, is how we have been making the finest carriages for the best people for over two hundred years."

"Most impressive," Ruby said, politely.

"We'll start you on the wheel joists," Matthew said to Ruby with a sniff. "They are easy and you will not be able to make too many mistakes. When you've mastered the joists, we'll look into moving you on to more complex pieces."

"Very well," said Ruby.

"As a junior polisher, your quota is twenty wheel joists a day," Matthew continued, "and that's the case whether the woodworkers send in ash or teak, even though teak is much harder to polish. This means that you need to learn how to work slowly when we're doing ash and quickly when we are doing teak. Twenty a day; no more and no less. Otherwise the whole system would fall apart. It might sound complicated and I can see that you are finding the whole thing a little intimidating. It is simpler than it sounds, though. You look like a bright girl; you'll get the hang of it quickly enough."

"Twenty a day whether it's fast or slow work? That doesn't make any sense!" Ruby protested. "Wouldn't..."

"It doesn't matter whether it makes sense or not," Matthew replied rather sharply. "And if you want to do well here, you should remember that it is not your place to complain or have ideas or make suggestions to your superiors at work. Especially, I might add, on your very first day. It is your job to polish and if you don't you'll be out on your ear! There is a way of doing things and it is our way and it is what you are expected to do. Is that clear?"

Ruby said nothing. She could not think of how to respond. Matthew seemed to be quite nice, so why was he being so aggressive? She picked up her coarse sandpaper and started to polish.

"Matthew's not that bad," a quiet voice told her as she worked. "It is just that he's a rules man. There are rules and we have to follow them. That's the way it has always been here and Matthew has been working here since he was fifteen years old; he is old school. This is an old school sort of place. Don't worry; you will get used to it. The rules will be second nature to you in no time and then you will be one of us!"

Ruby looked at her co-worker, who gave her a wink. "My name is Robert," he said. "I'm sure that you'll be happy here, at least until things get so bad that we have to close down. We're a friendly bunch down here in polishing."

"Is this factory doing well?" Ruby asked her neighbour quietly as they polished industriously, their heads bent over their work (it was a teak day). "It all looks so run-down and on the way in this morning I could not help noticing that most of the buildings seem to be full of unsold carriages. If that's the case, why all the insistence that we keep doing things the same way? It looks to me as though it might be time to instigate some major changes around here instead."

"Shhh," Robert told her swiftly, glancing anxiously around to see if anyone had overheard her. "We don't speak of such things in here. Only the Boss is allowed to talk about that side of the business. Talking down the business is a sacking offence!"

For the rest of the week, Ruby got on with her polishing while saying as little as possible, just quietly observing everything that went on around her. The work was tedious and repetitive in the extreme. This was the first time she had experienced such repetitive chores. As she grew used to it, she found it reasonably pleasant and she discovered that there was a certain satisfaction to be derived from doing the same thing, over and over again. Besides, as Ruby had remarked to the Boss when she had been interviewed for the position, she was certainly not afraid of hard work. There was a rhythm to the polishing that was quietly satisfying and the smell of the freshly cut wood and warm linseed oil was very agreeable. While Ruby's hands were kept busy with her labours, her mind was free to wander and there was certainly a lot here to think about.

Ruby noticed that, as Matthew said, on those days when the woodworkers sent in teak, everyone had to work very hard, while on those days when ash was brought in, they all slowed down and spent a lot of time chatting. Chatting was pleasant, yet going home after a full day of not really doing very much was strangely unsatisfying. Ruby was sure that there must be a better way of organising things. After Matthew's outburst on her first day at work, she was reluctant to speak out of turn before she had organised her thoughts.

At night, Ruby lay on her narrow bed in her simple room high above the fruit-and-vegetable market. She was still desperately lonely in the City, although she had started to become friendly with some of her fellow workers. She thought about her experience of travelling from the convent to where she was now, and she thought about the factory and the lengthy process of constructing a carriage. An idea began to form at the back of her brain, yet she could not quite access it. Finally, she fell into an uneasy sleep.

*"Ride the horse in the
direction that it is going."*
Werner Erhard

As the days passed and became weeks, Ruby continued to ponder what she saw every day in the factory. The more Ruby thought about it, the sillier the system at work seemed to be. She decided to have a word with Robert, the boy who sat next to her at the polishing table.

"You're right," Robert said. "It is a stupid system. We all think so, even the people who have been working here for years. They have a 'shape up or ship out' policy here. Nobody would dare to complain. Talking down the company…"

"I know," Ruby finished. "It's a sacking offence."

Ruby worked quietly for another week, considering her observations and comparing them to the things she knew from her earlier experiences. Then, one day, Mathew was out and she finally had an opportunity to state them. They were working with ash in the polishing department that day, so everyone was quite relaxed and a little bored, in the right frame of mind to listen to anyone who was prepared to be entertaining.

"Perhaps I can tell a story," Ruby suggested. "It might help us to pass the time."

"That's a good idea," said Iris, the oldest of the polishers. "We used to do that, years ago, before we were told to stop, because people were having too much fun and there was a risk that they would get distracted from what they were supposed to be doing. That was in the day of the Boss's father. He was a real stickler for discipline! Perhaps it is all right now. I am pretty sure that there are not any specific rules against it and, as far as I know, it's not a sacking offence."

"I know a very good story," Ruby said. "My great-grandmother told it to me, a long time ago, and it's still my favourite. I think you'll like it, so I'll tell you that one."

And so Ruby began:

***

This story did not take place today or yesterday. Rather it took place a long time ago when the carriages were not yet run by clockwork and this City was just a small fishing village on the edge of a great ocean with no dreams of grandeur or glory at all. In that little village, a humble workshop employed ten people to make small fishing boats and these people had never really spoken to teach other about what they did or whether they were doing it the right way.

One day, there was a knock at the door. The door opened by itself, as if by magic, and there stood a magician with an albino mouse perched on his shoulder and a stone in his hand.

"If I'm not mistaken," he said, "it must be nearly time for your lunch break and I would like to invite you all to share a delicious pot of Stone Soup with me..."

***

Everyone listened attentively as Ruby's gentle voice wove the narrative, making it seem as if it was happening before their very eyes. When the story was finished Iris, the oldest of the polishers, and the one to whom all the others routinely looked for leadership, was the first to speak.

"That's not a bad story," she said, putting down her tools and the piece that she was working on and fixing Ruby with a piercing look, "although you are not being very subtle. We do all know that things are not done as well here as they might be and despite the fact that we all have ideas about how things could be done more efficiently, nobody wants to be fired. I know that I don't, not at my age. Where else would I find work? So the thing is, nobody wants to be the first person to add something to your soup. This isn't the type of place where people make soup together; it never has been. This is the sort of place where we do what we are told or face the consequences. You should know by now that having ideas about different ways to do things is not a good system for getting ahead here. It is seen as talking down the company, and that's...well, you know what that means. So what do you suggest?"

"It seems to me," Ruby posited, "that we could start by polishing ten pieces each on teak days and thirty on ash days. This would spread the work more easily and as we would be working at a better pace, the quality of our work would surely be better, which in turn would mean less polishing at the final stage."

"And," said Robert, jumping in to support Ruby, "as Matthew is not here at present, this is the perfect time to try out our new system. If it doesn't work out, we will never have to say anything to him. If it does, we'll be talking about something that is more than just an idea."

Iris sighed. "All right," she said. "We'll see what we can do. And if Matthew asks, I did not approve of this new plan and I did not give my consent to it. I am not prepared to get in trouble for someone else's daring. Agreed?"

"Agreed," said Ruby bravely.

Everyone agreed that they would give Ruby's proposal a chance and by the end of the week the polishing department was producing better work than ever before, just as Ruby had hoped that it would. Simple as the changes had been, they were astonishingly effective. The carriage builders soon noticed that the pieces they were sent were smoother and better finished and they sent one of their number down to find out what had been going on.

"Interesting..." he said. "While you are making changes, we have a few suggestions to make. We didn't mention them before, as we were afraid that it would look as though we were talking down the company. The fact is, we've never been fond of linseed oil, as it brings our hands out in blisters and nobody likes the way it feels on their fingers. Olive oil is really better for this type of work..."

"Hmm," said Ruby. "I'd better check with the woodworkers if olive oil will do." She went down to the woodworking room and asked the woodworkers what they thought.

"We've always thought that olive oil would be better," the woodworkers said. "We were afraid to say anything. You know…"

"Yes, yes," said Ruby, a little impatiently. "You were afraid it might be a sacking offence. If you ask me, there's far too much talk about sacking in this factory!"

"Yes, well. If the change has been ordered by the higher-ups, then we are more than happy to accept it. Olive oil is cheaper, too, because it's produced locally in fields on the outskirts of the City. Linseed oil has to be brought in by catamaran from far away and it is a huge expense to the company. I don't know why we ever used it at all, to tell you the truth."

Matthew was sick for two weeks and when he came back the production area had been transformed and was working better and more efficiently than ever. A pleasant smell of warm olive oil filled the premises and the woodworkers' hands were soft and supple as never before (this was something that cheered up their spouses, too, and coming into work in a good mood as a result did not hurt their performance either).

With a weary sigh, Matthew called Ruby over for a word.

"Ruby," he said, quite kindly. "I have nothing against you. In fact, I like you very much. I see where you are coming from and I do appreciate that everyone is working more efficiently now than they were under the old system. Despite all that, I'm sorry to say that I am going to have to report you to the boss for insubordination and that means that you will almost certainly be sacked. Not doing that would mean that I wasn't doing my own work properly and that just wouldn't be right. Besides, it would mean that my job would be on the line and I don't want that either. Especially because I am the third generation of my family to work here and it means a lot to me. You understand."

"Very well," said Ruby bravely, although she did not feel nearly as brave as she sounded. Her brief forays into the City had made her realise that she was quite intimidated by the teeming masses of people, the shops bigger than temples and the traffic that seemed to be intent on colliding with passers-by. Work was not that easy to find and living all by herself in the small room overlooking the under-stocked fruit-and-vegetable market was really rather lonely and depressing, especially because there was no reliable way for her to send letters home or receive any back. She felt utterly cut off from everything and everyone she had ever known. Ruby sat down at her workstation and picked up a piece of teak. She started to polish it as best she could while she waited for her summons to the Boss's office, where she knew that she would hear her fate.

Once again, Ruby found herself in the room of the Boss. This time, although she was nervous, she was also determined to make her point. He turned around in his chair. He looked even crosser than before. His blue shirt was crumpled and his hair was on end, as if he had been furiously running his fingers though it - which was in fact the case. A heap of viciously twisted paperclips on his desk testified to his extremely bad mood.

"I hear you've been causing trouble in the polishing room," the Boss said, abruptly. "Trouble is not something that I can tolerate. So unless you can think of a good reason why I should keep you on, you are going to have to go. Whatever your name is."

"If I may," Ruby said. "I would like to address you by your name. I don't like talking to someone when I don't know his name."

"My name is John," the Boss said. "I mean, 'Mr. Smith'. You can call me 'Mr. Smith'."

> *"Do not speak harshly to any one; those who are spoken to will answer thee in the same way. Angry speech is painful: blows for blows will touch thee."*
> **Buddha**

"Well, John," Ruby said. "My name is 'Ruby' and you may call me 'Ruby.' When I started working here, I told you that I knew a lot about work. I believe that I also told you my name. Let's not worry about that for the time being. The fact is that while I still know relatively little about making carriages, I do know a lot about hard work. In fact, thanks to my experiences in the polishing room and to all the time that I have spent listening to the other workers, I know even more about this work and I can share some of my observations with you before you give me my marching papers."

"You produce fine carriages here," Ruby continued, "and it is certainly true that I don't know very much about carriages. In fact, I really don't know anything about them at all. I have only ever travelled in one once and an uncomfortable and expensive experience it certainly was. I am not going to pretend that I have a better technique for building carriages than the one that your factory has perfected in the course of making the finest carriages for the best people for two hundred years. I have worked, in the past, on a number of projects involving a large number of people and I do know more than a little about helping workers to organise themselves so that they can produce more efficiently and easily than before."

"You just don't get it, do you? That's why I can tell you that experience matters a lot more than enthusiasm. Efficiency of production is the very least of my problems," Mr. Smith said. "And I can show you why. Come with me."

He left the room, indicating that Ruby should follow him. And although the door almost swung closed in her face, she did.

Mr. Smith brought Ruby into a vast warehouse on the outer perimeter of the factory. He opened the door and stood back with an expansive gesture.

"Take a look for yourself, if you want to see why productivity is not the problem here."

Ruby took a step into the warehouse. It was huge, yet despite its size it was completely filled with carriages, each of which had been completed and polished to the very highest specifications. There were three-wheel and four-wheel carriages, wind-up clockwork carriages for short journeys, and sail-carriages for trips across the windswept desert. There were simple carriages for everyday use and ornate ones for formal occasions. There were black carriages for funerals and white ones for weddings. There were brand-new carriages that Ruby herself had worked on and older carriages, festooned with cobwebs, which had remained unsold for years. Every single bit of floor space was occupied. There were even a few of the lighter carriages hanging from the roof, suspended by joists, because the floor space was simply running out.

"Nobody is buying carriages anymore," Mr. Smith said gloomily. "They are very labour-intensive and the materials are costly, so that even if we sell them without making a profit, only the very rich can afford to buy them, and these days, even the rich are being very careful with their money. Unless we can improve our sales, we're going to be out of business very soon, so all your better efficiency in the polishing room is doing is giving me a headache. I just don't have the storage space for all the finished carriages and I don't have any extra money to spend on renting warehouses."

"I see," said Ruby. "Well, this is a problem."

"So will you go back to the old way of doing things?" Mr. Smith asked. "If you do, I will let you keep your job —at least until we have to wind things up here as I don't know how long I can keep everyone on and I hate to fire the people who worked with my father."

Ruby smiled and Mr. Smith took this to be her assent. Ruby knew, however, that she had not promised anything.

When Ruby returned to the polishing room, she found her colleagues huddled together. They turned around when she came in and looked at her with sympathy.

"We've put together a little collection," they said. "It is not much. It's all we have been able to manage. We hope that it will help you to get by until you find a new job. We like you, Ruby, and we are going to miss you, although you can't say we did not warn you that trouble was on the way when you started trying to change things around here."

"New job?" said Ruby. "I did not get fired. Thank you so much for your kindness and generosity. Really, I don't need any extra help, at least not for now."

Beneath their astonished gazes, she picked up a wheel joint and her polishing tools and returned to work.

Everyone stared at Ruby in sheer astonishment. This was the first time that anyone could remember a humble employee confronting the Boss and not getting sacked. In fact, thinking about it carefully, it was the first time that they remembered anyone confronting the Boss at all. Quickly, they all thought of the things that they had done or not done to avoid incurring his wrath. The older workers had been doing and not doing things to avoid being yelled at since back in the Boss's father's day. Many of the workers had sat uncomfortably with their legs crossed for hours so as to avoid going to the bathroom outside of scheduled breaks. Others had come into work when they were not feeling well. Several of the women had concealed their pregnancies until the last possible moment, because they were afraid that they would be seen as incapable of working. Nobody had ever dared pose an idea of their own. In fact, they had rather got out of the habit of having ideas of their own at all, because of the general fear that a new idea would be seen as a criticism of the old way of doing things which was, of course, seen as talking down the company and was therefore a sacking offence.

"What is more," Ruby said, apparently oblivious to their astonished expressions. "I bet we can find a way to make things really work around here. Let's all go home tonight and think about what we could do."

Then, although she knew that she was not supposed to, Ruby told everyone about the likelihood that the factory would soon close because people were not buying carriages any more. Nobody was really that surprised by this bad news. Despite the fact that nobody was allowed to say such things at work, they all had eyes in their heads and brains to think with. The stress of working in an apparently doomed enterprise had been weighing heavily on them all for quite some time.

> *"Close scrutiny will show that most 'crisis situations' are opportunities to either advance, or stay where you are."*
> **Dr Maxwell Maltz**

That was a long and sleepless night for all the workers and for Mr. Smith too. Then, in the morning, something wonderful happened. They started to make Stone Soup. People started to tell each other their ideas. They had always had ideas, of course. It was just that never before had they been brave enough to share them. Ruby's courage had shown them all that it was possible for them to say what they thought, after all.

The woodworkers said that they thought they would be very good at making school furniture, and one of them said that he knew how to make boats. Another said that he had been using the cast-off pieces for making toy carts for his little son.

"Toy carts," the head of the woodworking department said thoughtfully. "I have seen some of those little things go pretty fast. You should see my little boy go, when he starts at the top of a hill and gets the wind behind him."

The polishers said that they did not see the need for teak carriages at all. It was true that teak was a finer, more elegant wood that facilitated the carving of curlicues and folderols. There were plenty of elegant carriages carved from the finest teak gathering dust in the warehouse, while ash was so much easier to work. Ash carriages weighed less and moved more quickly, in any case. What was more, ash grew locally, whereas the teak had to be imported from overseas at considerable expense.

The carriage builders said that they had noticed that the blueprints they were using were terribly out of date.

Nobody wanted folderols and gilt on their carriages any more. Nowadays, it was all about clean, austere lines.

"We think," they said, "that it would be worth investing in some new designs. We're still making the same models that were created two hundred years ago. Since then, tastes and needs have changed."

"Hmm," said Ruby. "This is all very interesting. We need to discuss this with Mr. Smith."

"With the Boss?" the employees all said in one voice. "No way! We'll all be fired."

"Well then," Ruby said, "if the business is likely to close soon anyway, I don't have very much to lose. I'll do it myself. I have already come face to face with Mr. Smith more than once and survived the encounter. I am beginning to think that his bark is probably worse than his bite."

Ruby made her way to Mr. Smith's office once more, feeling considerably less nervous than she had the last time. She smiled at his white-haired secretary, while ignoring her cries that the Boss was not to be disturbed. Ruby knew that he was not really very busy. With a gentle rap on his door, she let herself in.

"Mr. Smith," she said. "We need to talk."

Mr. Smith spun around in his office chair and looked at Ruby with bloodshot eyes.

"Do we?" he said wearily. "Do I really need to talk to the most junior member of the company? Do I really need to set aside time to talk to someone who is about as welcome right now as a thorn in my foot? Well, I suppose I have nothing to lose. Just be quick and don't use up too much of my time. I am not a patient man and I am feeling especially impatient right now. And you do keep butting in with unasked for opinions. I have never seen anything quite like it."

"It is true," Ruby said, sitting down and making herself comfortable, "that I know nothing about carriages and that there are many fine people working here who do. However, despite my lack of knowledge of carriages, I believe that, with your leadership and some clever changes, this company could once again be successful. In fact, I am quite sure that it could be successful beyond your wildest dreams."

Ruby explained to Mr. Smith exactly what the woodworkers, polishers and carriage builders had told her.

"I don't understand," Mr. Smith said. "Why has nobody said anything to me before? If they were all unhappy about the way that things were being done, why didn't they tell me anything about it?

"They are all scared of you," was Ruby's simple reply. "They are afraid that if they say anything or even admit to having ideas that they will be fired."

"I am a fair man!" he protested. "I wouldn't fire someone for having an idea."

"You do give the impression of being rather cross," Ruby observed. "All this business of 'shape up or ship out' is quite intimidating and my great-grandmother used to say that if you go around saying angry things all the time pretty soon people know you as an angry person. I think that she just might have been right. Also, those poor, mutilated paperclips...they do make a person feel anxious. Not to mention the warning I hear all the time, that talking down the business, whatever that means, is a sacking offence."

"Huh," said Mr. Smith, hurriedly dropping the paperclip he had been twisting obsessively between his fingers. "I have just been doing things the way they've always been done around here."

"Indeed you have."

"If we don't make carriages," he said, "what are we to make? We have been producing the finest carriages in the country for over two hundred years. That is all we know how to do and we do it very well…"

"That," Ruby observed, "seems to be the problem."

"When a thing is new, people say 'It is not true.' Later, when its truth becomes obvious, they say 'It is not important.' Finally, when its importance cannot be denied, they say, 'Anyway, it is not new.'"
William James

Because Mr. Smith had plenty of time on his hands - he had sacked the sales team some time ago and was now handling the few sales there were by himself - he sat and listened to Ruby as she told him all about her experiences. She told him about the Land where she came from. She was sure that the Bureaucrat-in-Chief was still waiting for tourists to arrive to admire the Palace and buy the people's produce. Although Ruby had been sent into exile, she did not bear the citizens of her Land any ill-will and she was sure that their lives would be easier and more profitable if they had customers to buy their goods. Perhaps being less worried about money all the time would also make it easier for them to start questioning the wholly unreasonable rules that dominated their lives and maybe even move towards a better way of doing things.

"My Land is very far from here," she said. "And one of the reasons why it takes so long to reach is the fact that there are only two types of transport available. One can walk, as I did much of the way, which takes a very long time, is quite dangerous and extremely hard on even the most resilient footwear, or one can take a carriage, which is even slower, and terribly uncomfortable, what with having to stop to wind them up all the time, and so forth."

"Then," she said. "There is another Place that I know." Ruby told the Boss about the convent and all the fine produce that the nuns were able to grow and create on their land.

"I know for a fact," she said, "that they produce far more than they can ever eat. It was quite upsetting, watching them having to compost perfectly good fruits and vegetables. And I have also noticed how poor in quality the fruits and vegetables in the City are. My room here overlooks the fruit-and-vegetable market and most days the tables are largely empty. Even on a good day, you are lucky to find a bunch of softening carrots. Frankly, I'm surprised you don't all have rickets. If the nuns could only have access to an easier, faster way to transport their produce, it could be sold here. The carriages that go from there to here seem to be so badly constructed and slow that travel is very awkward and uncomfortable. It is really far from ideal for any market gardener who wants to bring goods to market and hopes for them still to be fresh when he arrives."

"What are you saying?"

"I'm suggesting that we switch to making carts in ash, which is faster and lighter, and stop making so many carriages, which nobody wants to buy, in any case. With the simpler, lighter vehicles for transporting people and produce…"

"Yes," said the Boss in a tone dripping with sarcasm. "I may not have your level of expertise, Ruby. Nonetheless, I have thought of that. The problem is that, in the City, times are not so good. Even the delivery people are not buying carts. How are we supposed to sell these famous carts when nobody has the money to buy them?"

Ruby looked at him with a gentle smile. Despite his crossness, she was beginning to feel quite fond of him.

I told you so, her great-grandmother whispered.

Oh, shut up, Ruby thought back.

"Oh, I wasn't thinking of selling the carts," Ruby said. "I thought we could start a delivery company using our own carts and carriages and we can even convert a lot of our current stock so we start with a large fleet. You see, if we can make fast, regular deliveries we can hire drivers from the City and take produce from the village where my friends the nuns live and sell it here and far away - wherever people need fresh fruit and vegetables. This way, we can use all of the existing staff to operate a business that provides what people really want, which is easier access to good quality, value for money, products and produce. The carts would enable the business to grow, rather than being an end in themselves, and if we other businesses see our success and contribute as well, we can lift the whole city up."

As Ruby told her story about a profitable transport business that also made its own means of transport, the Boss visibly shifted and a light came into his eye. The vision took hold and the expression on his face changed dramatically as the wheels turned in his mind.

"Either you are completely mad or we both are. Or perhaps you're a genius and you have just given me the perfect way to turn this factory around! So what the hey - let's do it!" the Boss cried, as he left the office.

"And," he added, turning around quickly so as to hold the door and prevent it from closing in Ruby's face, "you can call me 'John'."

You know, my dear, Ruby's great-grandmother whispered. *I think that John just might be the one for you.*

Nonsense, Ruby thought, quite firmly, and put an end to that.

There were still some barriers to cross. The business had long relied on a small set of suppliers for their teak, ash, and oil and these suppliers were used to filling the same order every month.

"I can't just change everything," one owner protested. "We've always supplied equal parts of ash and teak. How do you expect me to change my systems? It will mean a complete overhaul and that is really the last thing I need to worry about in difficult times like these! We've been supplying the carriage business for generations; our methods have always worked before and we are not going to change them now."

"I'm afraid you will have to change," Ruby explained. "Especially if you want to keep us as a customer. We just don't have that much time to wait. Things are hard in the City in general, as you know, so we will need to move very fast to keep our heads above water."

There was a certain amount of grumbling. After Ruby had listened to objection after objection, she had a real sense of how the man felt; he was getting older and he had been doing the same thing for many decades. It would be hard for him to change. At the same time, he seemed to be coming to quite like her, despite what she saw as her unreasonable requests. Without letting the way he felt dissuade her from her path, Ruby began to have a degree of empathy for the older man. Eventually the supplier talked himself out and reluctantly agreed to Ruby's plain request for a test batch. She had asked him for something that she felt he could give in order to open the doorway to a longer cooperation. Ruby went back to the factory with the good news.

Although the supplier continued to insist that he was going to come up with the goods, they just did not come on time. This caused serious problems to the new business that Ruby had proposed. For a whole week, the builders and polishers and makers sat twiddling their thumbs because they did not have any ash to work with. Everyone grew very anxious about this situation and they began to doubt their capacity to even be involved with a new enterprise. Even if the carriage-making industry had not been doing any business, at least they knew where they stood with it.

"It's not my fault that we haven't been able to give you what you ask for," the supplier said. "We're doing our best; it's not easy, integrating a whole new way of doing things."

"I understand," Ruby said. "The problem here is that you're causing us serious difficulties and if things continue like this, we are going to run into trouble. As you know, we're launching a new range of products and services, we've already invested a lot of money in advertising and promotion and we really need to stay on schedule or all that money will be wasted. Unless you can start delivering on time, we might have to look for a new supplier who can give us what we need, when we need it."

"Are you sure it's the right time to launch anything? I mean, the company's so good at making carriages. They've been making the best carriages for the finest people for over two hundred years, you know."

"Yes, I know," said Ruby. "And now we are doing something else. And you are really going to have to start giving us what we need when we need it."

*"Imagination is the beginning of creation.
You imagine what you desire, you will
what you imagine, and at last you
create what you will."*
George Bernard Shaw

Ruby noticed that the owner of the supplier was becoming quite angry with her, although she was doing her very best to be polite and to explain everything as clearly and patiently as she could muster. He seemed to think that she was insulting him and his work, rather than simply asking him for something new. This put Ruby in a very difficult situation indeed. Despite her fine words about finding another supplier, Ruby knew that the man standing before her was the only provider in town. This also meant that she could not afford to antagonise him, leaving them at a very awkward impasse. She went back to the factory to see if she could come up with an idea.

Ruby discussed the situation with John, who did not have any smart ideas either. John was used to running the business the way it had been; he had never had to do anything new before and he did not find it particularly easy to wriggle out of the groove he had always worked in. Because of the transportation problem, suppliers were far and few between and there were few choices. Ruby and John returned to the supplier to see if they could unite their efforts to improve the situation.

"We've been buying teak from you for many years…" John started. "Some teak and ash…"

"That's right," the owner said. "Teak is a fantastic material. We've always concentrated most of our efforts on teak, which has been used to make the finest carriages for the finest people for more than two hundred years!"

"The thing is," Ruby said gently, "now that we are changing things around at the factory, we need to work mostly with ash, not teak. Ash is light, which is what we need for making our new carts. And people today don't need the same things as people needed two hundred years ago. We are phasing out carriages and focusing on creating the sort of transport system that this City really requires."

"Huh. Ash, you say? A rather feeble sort of wood, I have always thought. Not really worth bothering with, if you want my opinion."

The supplier was obviously not happy about Ruby's request for ash. The fact was, he made a lot more money from working teak. While it was true that it was harder to work, it was not as much harder as he said and the profit margins were a great deal higher with teak.

"I can't help noticing," Ruby said, changing tack for a moment, "that there seem to be a lot of unfinished pieces lying about the ash section of the factory. Do you have some sort of problem with your production line?"

"Problem? No, not at all. No problems here."

Despite several visits, Ruby wasn't making any progress.

Dejected, Ruby finally left. She went to talk to her friends in the polishing department and asked them what they thought was going on. They had all known the supplier for many years; perhaps they would be able to give her some fresh insight into what might be going on in his mind.

"You know," Mathew said thoughtfully. "It might be something very simple. Sometimes the simplest things can be the most difficult to see. It very well may be that the owner of the supply company wants to sell more teak because they charge more for it and make more money on each sale."

That night, Ruby dreamed of her great-grandmother and when she awoke she felt sure that she had the answer to the problem with the supplier. So, in the morning, she asked John to come with her to see him. On their, she filled John in on what she thought might be the best way to fix things. John concurred with Ruby's analysis of the situation and, between them, they approached the younger manager of their teak production line and asked him to set up his own ash parts production company so that they would have a supplier on whom they could rely. This was something that he was more than qualified to do, and soon the problem of supplies had been solved.

By the end of the month the factory was making simple, light carts to sell within the City and to export to neighbouring lands, including Ruby's own Land, and that in which she had met the nuns. Before long, the company was known everywhere for providing a reliable service for the transport of just about anything between one land and another. Soon, the fruit-and-vegetable market in the City had much more to offer, the factory was creating a handsome profit and a few tourists even braved the arduous visa requirements to visit the Bureaucrat-in-Chief's Palace. On the streets of the City, the level of cursing declined rapidly as, one-by-one, carriage drivers learned how to manage the new vehicles. And that was not all. Ruby had found that, behind the brusque façade, John was a kind and gentle man who had simply needed the opportunity to reveal his true self.

A year to the day after Ruby's arrival in the City, she and John were married and shortly thereafter Ruby was pleased to announce to all her friends in the factory that they were expecting their first child. She could not have been happier. How good life was! How lucky Ruby was! Surely, nothing bad was ever going to happen to this most blessed couple.

Ruby joined John in the company, which they now ran together as it expanded and grew. While they had their occasional disagreements, for the most part they were a perfect working team in the factory and at home and, while many people say that it is not good to work together and live together, Ruby and John seemed blissfully ignorant of this. They were a perfect team. Ruby had a real instinct for business and a deep knowledge of the workings of the human mind and John was a master at putting her inspiration to work. Together, they inspired their workers to explore and improve their work. They treated them with integrity and were rewarded with a loyal workforce and a happy customer base.

The City in which they lived was not perfect, yet it was full of opportunity and it was a good place with many fine inhabitants. All in all, it seemed to be a good place to settle down, run a business and raise a family, and they had no regrets and few doubts about the marvellously entwined life upon which they had embarked. Ruby had not dreamed, on that dark day when she was banished from her Land, that so much happiness lay ahead. She could never have imagined that, together with her kind, handsome husband, she would be running such an interesting, successful organisation. However, Ruby's journey through life was far from over; many adventures still lay ahead and not all of them were happy ones.

Lessons from
Wheels Within Wheels

In the real world, as in Ruby's story, businesses often reach an impasse when what they are producing, doing or offering is no longer what people are looking for. When this happens, there can be a crisis or there can be an opportunity. Clearly, there is an urgent need for change. It is important to understand and appreciate that needing to change the way one does things or what one's products are is not a value judgement on the organisation, rather, it is a reflection of our evolving society.

It is extremely important to recognise when change is needed before not changing becomes a problem. Think about the needs of a growing child. When a baby is just beginning to learn how to crawl, he has no idea that touching something hot will hurt him or that playing with sharp carving knives is maybe not the best idea for someone of his size and stature. Fortunately, you are there all the time to pick him up whenever he starts to crawl towards the fire and to make sure that the sharp knives are stored where he cannot reach. While you can prevent your baby from playing with fire, the cautious approach will not always work - hopefully you will not have to manhandle your eighty kilo teenage son away from the fire before he hurts himself! Somewhere between infancy and adolescence, your child will have learned for himself the importance of staying away from very hot objects and of treating sharp knives with care.

In a talk featured on TED.com[6] Gever Tulley, founder of the Tinkering School, spells out five dangerous things you should let your kids do, including playing with knives. As he says, the young heal faster than the old. In our changing society, smart organisations react to what people need and reorganise or change what they offer in terms of goods or services accordingly. In other words, they take on some risk now so as to succeed later and, just as we are over-allergic to risk regarding our kids and sharp things, companies tend to become more allergic to risk the more successful they become. Change can be stressful and difficult, calling for us to assess and explore our very identities. Imagine the upheavals that must have taken place at lamp-makers' workshops around the world as electricity gradually delivered light to an increasing number of homes. A million lamp-makers must have had to think, "Well, if I cannot be a lamp-maker, what am I then?" The smart ones will have decided that they could deliver this new-fangled electricity or open the gift shop they had always dreamt of owning and so forth. In the process of making change, one needs to accept that there may be feelings of stress and even grief as old ways of doing things are laid to rest. It is normal and natural to mourn what is gone and fear one's ability to broach the new and unfamiliar; accepting this as true makes it easier to move forward with a new plan.

Throughout our lives, we learn by comparing new experiences to past experience. A baby will learn to recognise the face of her mum and dad by seeing them every day and gradually memorising the features of their faces and the sounds of their voices. As we grow

---

[6] www.ted.com/talks/gever_tulley_on_5_dangerous_things_for_kids.html

up, we all refer to what we have experienced to make decisions. The familiar becomes our template for what we should do and how we should do it. In many situations, this works out very well. Indeed, the more we use any circuit in our brain the more it gets insulated with myelin and the faster the circuit becomes. However, there are also times when we need to enable ourselves to break away from the old and do something new, even though we know that there is a risk that it will not work out.

You may be sure that when Gutenberg started printing copies of his Bible on the world's first commercial printing press back in 1455, plenty of his friends and acquaintances told him that people had been buying hand-written texts since time immemorial and that interest in printed books would be limited. No doubt there were plenty of people at the time who were prepared to stand around and scoff at his foolishness. Conversely, we do not need to go so far back in time to look at business predictions that have been badly off-target such as Bill Gates famously predicting that the Internet would never really take off. While there are certainly many more examples of initiatives that were taken and that did not go anywhere, when something new fills a need that previously went unfilled, success is inevitable.

Often the repercussions of innovations can go way beyond the market and even beyond the imaginations of the inventors. Think, just for example, about the explosion in domestic appliances in the nineteenth and twentieth centuries. Washing machines, electric ovens, vacuum cleaners and all the other items that are now basic and expected in every home in the developed world were once innovations that made a lot of money for their creators. They also facilitated the revolutionary movement that saw women in many countries begin to take their places in the public forum, thanks in very large part to a reduction in the need for back-breaking work in the home. Although they probably never expected it, those inventors played a crucial role in one of the biggest social revolutions the world has ever seen.

Many innovators fail the first and even the second or third time they try something new. This is normal and even healthy; what is not healthy is never even trying something new. Success nearly always comes because of a series of iterations during which things are refined until they work. It is clear why persistent optimists are better candidates to be innovators (innovation is, incidentally, often the combination of two or more existing ideas that have been "borrowed" and put together in a new way). Pessimistic predictions are rarely useful in innovation, even though they may be essential in other areas. For instance, jet engine mechanics can always do with a dose of pessimism to ensure that all the bad things that can happen have been thought of and accounted for. To really innovate, it is necessary to accept that there will be failure along the way, to understand, appreciate and accept that everything is not going to be completely perfect and flawless the first time it is attempted. There is no shame in failing, if we understand that a "failure" is an attempt on the way to achievement. Understanding that we will never get everything right the first time or even the second or third time we try is a very important aspect of success. Great achievers are not afraid to take risks, in full knowledge of the fact that at least some of their risks will not work out.

Being adaptable to change is not only something that must be addressed on a personal level, it is also something that should be considered in terms of the make-up of your enterprise. I have worked with a lot of software developers and have seen a lot of start-ups turn into businesses, and then corporations. Through these experiences, one error I have seen repeated is to outnumber the productive doers, people who are both physically and mentally creative, who actually build something other people use, with less productive talkers, especially in software development. I have found, with software in particular, that the ideas generated internally tend to dilute the value proposition to the customer. I am now convinced that the number of engineers, developers, creative-types and support people should be a multiple of the number of administration, marketing and sales staff. I'm including customer support as creatives for their vital role in feeding customers' problems and complaints back into production. In any organisation, as in Ruby's factory, where most of the employees left are doers – engineers who make the carriages there should be more doers than anyone else. With such a structure, the light weight of the infrastructure allows the company to be agile and change what it is doing easily.

A RECIPE FOR STONE SOUP

One generous portion of belief

One or more enthusiastic catalysts

One well defined context, communicated well

Testing for bad eggs so that you can leave them out

A heaping spoonful of emotion and trust

The ability to react proportionately and
level-headedly in times of crisis or change

A triple dose of reality

A preheated holistic present

A substantial dollop of perspective

A variety of questions including
self-questioning without self-doubt

Several spoonfuls of leadership
gravitas steeped in female energy

A large measure of inspiration fortified by deep listening

An embrace of change

Coup d'oeil, literally "the strike of an eye," is a term that was coined by Napoleon referring to the ability of truly successful military commanders to use their instincts to evaluate the battlefield, recognise opportunity and seize the opportune moment to achieve a great victory. Attributing this to instinct makes it sound easy, yet what is needed is more a heady combination of strategic intuition and situational awareness. The same term has been applied to business and is exemplified in Ruby's ability to evaluate the current state of the factory, recognise opportunity and seize the moment to save it from its impending demise. Successful business people master the art of taking in the wider picture at a glance, giving them sudden flashes of inspiration that show them the right course of action to take. Such flashes must have been behind the foundation of some of the world's most successful enterprises, when a potential need was spotted and filled.

As well as being able to see the bigger picture in terms of the context of your business, it is also important to see the bigger picture in terms of the larger world and your place in it. Seeing the bigger picture allows you to consider your basic principles and values and incorporate them into the plan for how you will operate both on a daily and a longer term basis. As members of a global community, we all have responsibilities. At the same time, when you contribute on a large scale it creates opportunities for your business that would not otherwise be available. Also in my view the path of the entrepreneur is actually a powerful weapon to combat poverty. Indeed, just as an entrepreneur in the developed world must first strive in order to thrive, so people in the developing world can benefit from the same strategy.

The word "poverty" is commonly heard on the news or in socially conscious circles and most of us probably feel confident that we know what it means, yet it is not as simple as it seems. Around the world, unfortunately, there are countless millions of people who live every day of their lives without knowing where their next meal will come from or how to access a clean glass of water. In what is generally known as the "developed" world, there are also many people whose living situations would be considered to be impoverished. In countries with a developed welfare system, these people are not likely to have serious issues with lack of access to food and safe drinking water, and yet they still experience the uncertainty and anxiety associated with poverty.

Poverty is not just a lack of access to material resources. It is also often comes with a lack of self-worth, a feeling that one is profoundly unequal to other members of society and unable to improve one's own lot. It is the feeling that there is no point in even trying, because one is bound to fail anyway. In fact, there are, by some measures, greater levels of despair and misery in more developed societies as opposed to less, because in great part of the associated envy and anxiety in communities with an unequal distribution of wealth.

To be serious about helping people out of poverty, we need to realise that the relatively quick fix of just giving food or money often does long term harm. Much more important than an injection of resources is the provision of belief in a future, the expectation of achievement and the means to change one's situation for oneself, indeed the very belief in something worth striving for. There are a lot of people in the world who ask themselves what they can do to help make the world a better place and then, unintentionally, go on to do something that garners the exact opposite result, harm because of the unintended consequences. For example, I once met a very poor Ugandan man. Through an interpreter, he told me that he was from the north of the country, that he used to be a farmer and that his family had farmed for generations. I asked whether the war that had recently affected his region had destroyed his farm. His response was to vehemently deny this suggestion and state that the cause of the loss of his livelihood was very clear. He had been driven out of business because he could not sell his crops as a result of all the surplus food that had been dumped in his region by aid agencies working by donation quotas. Wealthy aid-giving countries generally have the best of good intentions, yet those good intentions can lead to disastrous results. In this case, they had reduced this hard-working farmer and his family to penury.

If you, like me, ask the question, "What can I contribute?" the temptation is often to immediately supply the answer yourself. This is an exercise in well-intentioned arrogance and is a mistake that I see happening time and time again in many contexts. This is the usual motivation behind charity, which is well-intentioned, yet often less than helpful. I see this sort of arrogance in leaders, in catalysts and in those who are rigorously bureaucratic. It is very insidious because it allows someone to be supremely well-intentioned and to feel justified while ruining another person's day, career or even life. It is only in taking the time to see the bigger picture, not just how we fit in it, also what the realities are for the people we want to help, that we can truly begin to be of real assistance. If we wish to assist people to do more than merely survive we need to inspire them to strive and thereby thrive just as any good entrepreneur does.

A RECIPE FOR STONE SOUP
One generous portion of belief

One or more enthusiastic catalysts

One well defined context, communicated well

Testing for bad eggs so that you can leave them out

A heaping spoonful of emotion and trust

The ability to react proportionately and
level-headedly in times of crisis or change

A triple dose of reality

A preheated holistic present

A substantial dollop of perspective

A variety of questions including
self-questioning without self-doubt

Several spoonfuls of leadership
gravitas steeped in female energy

A large measure of inspiration fortified by deep listening

An embrace of change

A view of the bigger picture

We are all much worse at multitasking than we think. New research shows that driving while talking on the phone is more dangerous than drink driving even when using a hands-free device. It makes you wonder how much quality attention is being destroyed by people attending important meetings with their Blackberry. In order to be a catalyst you need to be able to give someone your undivided attention for as long as it takes in order to determine the real issue they are presenting. Oftentimes people will bring you a side issue and not tell you their main issue immediately. If you focus too much on trying to save time, you may end up missing the whole point. There have been several occasions when I have found myself sitting in important meetings listening carefully while others allowed themselves to be distracted by daydreaming or using their Blackberries. After such encounters, I have often found myself to be the only one to have a full recollection of the meeting and I have been able to use this to my advantage. In these situations, I have often been able to pick up insights that others missed because they were bored and distracted and have been able to form closer bonds with people "on the other side of the table" because of my focussed attention. While I was gaining much information of strategic value by being attentive, I was making a positive impression on those doing the talking as others find being really listened to be both flattering and rewarding, as Ruby demonstrated in listening to her co-workers. Who does not like to know that his or her insights, ideas and issues are being given the attention they deserve?

I experienced the counterpoint of this example in one particular high-level meeting I attended in an investment bank. Upon walking into the room, I was offered a cup of coffee. I declined and asked for water. Seconds later the same person asked, "Coffee, wasn't it?"

Puzzled, I answered, "No, water will be fine, thank you."

I then received a coffee cup and was asked, "Cream or Sugar?"

At that point, I was already quite incredulous and it was only the start of the meeting.

We all need to know that we are being listened to. Whenever you encounter a new business or indeed an organisation of any type, look at how the "lesser" members are treated by management. If they are not listened to and treated with dignity and respect, how much emphasis do you think that organisation places on listening?

A RECIPE FOR STONE SOUP

One generous portion of belief

One or more enthusiastic catalysts

One well defined context, communicated well

Testing for bad eggs so that you can leave them out

A heaping spoonful of emotion and trust

The ability to react proportionately and
level-headedly in times of crisis or change

A triple dose of reality

A preheated holistic present

A substantial dollop of perspective

A variety of questions including
self-questioning without self-doubt

Several spoonfuls of leadership
gravitas steeped in female energy

A large measure of inspiration fortified by deep listening

An embrace of change

A view of the bigger picture

Patience and presence

Although she may not realise it yet, we already know that Ruby is truly an entrepreneur. It's just a matter of time before she starts putting her abilities into action.

What is an entrepreneur? And what makes them different to other types of people? Can anyone just decide to be an entrepreneur? Do you have what it takes?

Sarasvanthy[7] believes that entrepreneurs have cracked what she refers to as "effectual reasoning," which she believes to be the opposite of causal reasoning. The latter depends on measurables such as a targets, goals and systems, whereas effectual reasoning

---

[7] Sarasvanthy, 2001.

refers to working with a "given set of means" while allowing goals to "emerge contingently over time from the varied imagination and diverse aspirations of the founders [of an organisation] and the people they interact with." The best entrepreneurs are capable of both causal and effectual reasoning. Effectual reasoning is creative in and of itself. Sarasvanthy says that, "effectual reasoning demands something more - imagination, spontaneity, risk-taking, and salesmanship." These are all traits that Ruby has already demonstrated in abundance. In her research, Sarasvanthy interviewed a large number of entrepreneurs of diverse types. She discovered that they tended to "find ways to reach the market with minimum expenditure of resources such as time, effort, and money," and that they were generally able to "turn the unexpected into the profitable." Effectual reasoning assumes that, as we can control the future with our own decisions and actions, we do not need to predict it.

A RECIPE FOR STONE SOUP

One generous portion of belief

One or more enthusiastic catalysts

One well defined context, communicated well

Testing for bad eggs so that you can leave them out

A heaping spoonful of emotion and trust

The ability to react proportionately and
level-headedly in times of crisis or change

A triple dose of reality

A preheated holistic present

A substantial dollop of perspective

A variety of questions including
self-questioning without self-doubt

Several spoonfuls of leadership
gravitas steeped in female energy

A large measure of inspiration fortified by deep listening

An embrace of change

A view of the bigger picture

Patience and presence

Effectual reasoning

I suspect if a long term study was carried out on leaders and managers who use fear and greed to get their way all the time, there would be some pretty revealing personal medical results. It's very stressful creating that sort of psychological environment! A persistent view states that one needs to be tough to succeed in business. I would say that you can be tough and succeed, however what you really need to consistently succeed is a complex balance of determination, leadership, teamwork and productivity. I see plenty of very smart people who are failures and also plenty of tough people who never amounted to anything.

Over the years, many people have told me that you need to use both a carrot and a stick to get things done as a leader. For a long time, I did not understand this analogy at all. In my mind's eye, I pictured a carrot tied to a stick hanging in front of a donkey. It was only later, when I saw a practitioner of this philosophy berating a helpless staff member, that I realised that the stick was supposed to be for threatening people with! Horrified, I vowed never to use such tactics to coerce people into action, because I can no longer see any circumstance in which threatening co-workers or employees is an appropriate action to take. In fact, for many years, I worked only on the carrot premise and often wondered why that did not seem to work all the time, either. In fact, some of the worst results I produced in the past were with the use of a carrot and stick approach before I understood its drawbacks.

It turns out that science has a better answer to both issues. When we are focussed on a task because of either fear or greed, we develop tunnel vision. This means that while you can use a carrot and/or a stick to motivate people to do more simple tasks, because of its basic, elementary nature, the very motivator you are using directly interferes to a very considerable extent with the higher capacities of passion and reason. You need only to look at the size of the bonuses paid to top investment bankers prior to the financial unpleasantness of the first decade of the third millennium to see that the size of the incentive does not guarantee proportionate performance. Only inspiration, determination and a sense of achievement can really motivate human beings to do more - especially if it is to do more with less. And this is a good reason why entrepreneurs and would-be entrepreneurs with inspiration, determination and a sense of achievement have good reason to feel optimistic, even in embattled times. The source of determination is often thought of as intrinsic - some people somehow being born with more than others - yet I have found that determination can be stimulated very simply by leading by example so that when you show your own determination it is far more likely to appear in the people you work with. So rather than contriving complicated incentives, lead by example and never give up!

A Recipe for Stone Soup

One generous portion of belief

One or more enthusiastic catalysts

One well defined context, communicated well

Testing for bad eggs so that you can leave them out

A heaping spoonful of emotion and trust

The ability to react proportionately and
level-headedly in times of crisis or change

A triple dose of reality

A preheated holistic present

A substantial dollop of perspective

A variety of questions including
self-questioning without self-doubt

Several spoonfuls of leadership
gravitas steeped in female energy

A large measure of inspiration fortified by deep listening

An embrace of change

A view of the bigger picture

Patience and presence

Effectual reasoning

Determination

Farhad Manjoo has written a fascinating book about how the information that is "out there" interacts with our perceptions of what is true and what is not. In the contemporary world, there are so many sources of "news" that we can always find ideas and reports that coincide with the worldview that we already have. Even in Ruby's world, as we have seen, people pick the reigning ideas that coincide most neatly with the assumptions that they already hold. At the same time, perception is the story we tell ourselves about how things "really" are and, often, perception is more important to us than reality. Indeed, this is so true that altering perceptions can alter effective reality. At a recent TED Global talk[8] Roy Sutherland, an executive with the advertising firm Ogilvy, presented an alternative case for what he would have done to improve passenger journeys on the Eurostar cross channel train. Engineers had recently spent six billion pounds on new works to reduce the journey time from London to Paris by forty minutes. Our man from Ogilvy suggested that, instead, they might have spent half that much to bring the world's top supermodels in to hand out complementary champagne for the journey over the next twenty years and then spent the other three billion on something else. For my part I think that, under those circumstances, I would ask the train to slow down a bit. At the very least I would have forgone 5.8 of the six billion and settled for free wifi on the train. Certainly, too, the question Lolita had asked me, discussed in the first chapter of this book, altered my view of the "reality" of who I was to great effect. What question do you need to ask to end up with a new reality for yourself?

---

[8] www.ted.com

A Recipe for Stone Soup

One generous portion of belief

One or more enthusiastic catalysts

One well defined context, communicated well

Testing for bad eggs so that you can leave them out

A heaping spoonful of emotion and trust

The ability to react proportionately and
level-headedly in times of crisis or change

A triple dose of reality

A preheated holistic present

A substantial dollop of perspective

A variety of questions including
self-questioning without self-doubt

Several spoonfuls of leadership
gravitas steeped in female energy

A large measure of inspiration fortified by deep listening

An embrace of change

A view of the bigger picture

Patience and presence

Effectual reasoning

Determination

An understanding that perception
is mutable and reality is not

After an insight has been realised or a discovery made, it often seems strangely obvious and we wonder how on earth it could have taken so long to reach that point. Van Hecke refers to these instances as 'blind spots'[9]. She believes that even very clever, successful people often tend to have bias and to jump to conclusions. We all

---

[9] Hecke, 2007.

need to learn how to be open to new suggestions and ways of doing things.

A RECIPE FOR STONE SOUP

One generous portion of belief

One or more enthusiastic catalysts

One well defined context, communicated well

Testing for bad eggs so that you can leave them out

A heaping spoonful of emotion and trust

The ability to react proportionately and
level-headedly in times of crisis or change

A triple dose of reality

A preheated holistic present

A substantial dollop of perspective

A variety of questions including
self-questioning without self-doubt

Several spoonfuls of leadership
gravitas steeped in female energy

A large measure of inspiration fortified by deep listening

An embrace of change

A view of the bigger picture

Patience and presence

Effectual reasoning

Determination

An understanding that perception
is mutable and reality is not

Strategic insight

Changing the way one does things is often hard, as we have all seen. It calls for learning to interpret new facts, rather than just repeating them and for recognising when it is important to use change to allow for the growth of your employees, not just your bottom line. In any novel situation, it is important to reward achievement and accountable behaviours and to keep the channels of communication open.

While embracing novelty, it helps to take little steps such as writing down goals. Did you know that the 5% of people who write down their goals are notably more successful than the other 95%, simply because they are much more likely to remember and thereby honour them? When a leader or catalyst is seen to honour their goals, it is easier for staff to honour theirs, as they must. The wisdom of this statement is so clear to me that I have spent many years refining a time management system based on goals that I use myself.

Goals come in various types, though we usually only think about short, medium and long term goals. I prefer to work in terms of open and closed goals, as well as considering whether my goals are extrinsic, altruistic or philanthropic goals or intrinsic or hedonistic personal goals. I also keep my goals in a hierarchy with open altruistic ones dominant over closed and hedonistic goals. I write my goals in my calendar rather than in a to-do list. I share my goals with people and am also very happy to take other people's worthy goals and set them for myself. At the top of my goal hierarchy is "a world that works for everyone." This is certainly not an original aspiration. It is one that I have borrowed and towards which I am genuinely working in everything I do. In fact, writing this book is part of this goal, as I want other people to benefit from the ideas it contains. This is my highest level goal. It is open, as it is something to be strived towards and not attained. It is extrinsic, as it is for the largest number of people possible. I am happy to share it and to know that it inspires people around me. Underneath it I have some intrinsic open goals, such as always striving to be fit and healthy while having fun. All of these support me in my top goal. I have many closed goals of both the intrinsic and extrinsic kind scattered in my calendar with a slight bias towards the extrinsic, as I know that my greatest satisfaction comes from being of service to others.

This system works just as well for companies as it does for individuals. The high level goals replace the ubiquitous mission and vision statements, the definitions of which are often lost in mindless bureaucracy. All my closed goals are measured against my open goals so that I am never in conflict with myself and they all have start and delivery dates as well as measurements. Since I have been working this way, I have become fantastically productive! While change and innovation may also call for the change and restructuring of previous goals, taking the time to rewrite them and plot the steps to their realisation can go a long way in helping you to make necessary adjustments when the time comes for change.

A RECIPE FOR STONE SOUP

One generous portion of belief

One or more enthusiastic catalysts

One well defined context, communicated well

Testing for bad eggs so that you can leave them out

A heaping spoonful of emotion and trust

The ability to react proportionately and
level-headedly in times of crisis or change

A triple dose of reality

A preheated holistic present

A substantial dollop of perspective

A variety of questions including
self-questioning without self-doubt

Several spoonfuls of leadership
gravitas steeped in female energy

A large measure of inspiration fortified by deep listening

An embrace of change

A view of the bigger picture

Patience and presence

Effectual reasoning

Determination

An understanding that perception
is mutable and reality is not

Strategic insight

Personal and group goals created, shared and honoured

The world economy has evolved. It started off with manufacturing and has changed in such a way that services are also an important component. As the world economy continues to evolve, there will be new experiences and products. For now, it is nearly always more profitable to deliver what people really want. In the case of Ruby and John's factory, nobody wanted carriages anymore in the City that Ruby made her home. Instead of making a single product better, the company was more successful when it switched to providing fast, reliable transport.

Often, people and organisations are so bent on producing something that they forget where real value lies. More and more businesses have moved down the so-called value chain, going from manufacturing to services to increase their profits and even from services to experiences and finally to the attention economy[10]. Nowadays, companies are realising that they need to look at the relationship economy as well as the network economy. These are new terms that embody the social connectedness of both suppliers and customers beyond their attention. If you can determine the end point value of people's needs and desires, there is a host of ways that can open up to deliver it. For example, long ago, people purchased raw wheat for their baking needs. At some point, you could pay to have your wheat hulled for you. Eventually you could buy flour, then bread, then sliced bread, then branded sliced bread, then home delivered organic bake-it-yourself bread. Of course by now you could also buy advertising for bread. Fresh warm bread also became part of the high class dining experience and now you can even buy virtual bread as part of some online multiplayer games to share with your virtual online friends. In each case the profit margin and therefore your position on the value chain increased. The profit margin on a virtual loaf of bread is almost 100%. By being open to

---

[10] "Attention is focused mental engagement on a particular item of information. Items come into our awareness, we attend to a particular item, and then we decide whether to act." (Davenport & Beck 2001, p. 20)

change and receptive of the changing needs of your customers, you can continue to build upon your success.

Many people are familiar with the term "salami tactics." The term brings to mind the image of breaking problems down into smaller manageable parts to tackle them. This is a very useful, valid approach to getting things done. Anyone in business should be sensitive to looking at complex issues this way and it is a very useful tool for making real achievements. What the catalyst needs to be able to do is take this skill to another level.

People are very good at unintentionally creating catch 22 situations. These occur in a variety of ways and can quickly build to a point of apparent insolubility. What is important to know about catch 22 situations is that one or more illogical ideas are woven into the problem and these ideas are often from diverse contexts. A lot of catch 22 situations fall into the class of problems that I call "chicken and scrambled egg problems." The first thing a catalyst should remember when faced with the apparently unsolvable is that if human beings create something apparently unmovable they can also unmake it and usually they can do this of their own volition. The world is full of examples of people faced with apparently hopeless situations who have managed, by carefully working with the people around them, to come out of even certain death with a future much brighter than that first imagined.

Instead of looking at a problem as a whole, the trick is to first look at it in smaller pieces to see which part you can solve easily because, more often than not, the biggest issue in tackling these situations is that no one wishes to begin working on the problems in the first place. Anyone you ask will happily tell you why what you wish to tackle is impossible. It may well be that, when you start actually taking action, perceived, imagined and even described potential difficulties start to melt away. There is something about starting to think about what you need to do and making a short list that makes the insurmountable suddenly look possible. In my experience, the sooner you can begin taking concrete actions and getting results (even small progress in the face of daunting tasks) the exponentially closer you are to achieving a resolution.

In dealing with seemingly insurmountable problems, I always recommend that people focus on the parts that they know how to get done, as the real secret to untying the Gordian knot is to keep your senses tuned while you work on it. Many of the issues that hold you up are only held in place by conventions or other people's emotional attachments to things being a certain way. Layer enough of these problems into the path of what you are trying to achieve and, quite quickly, it all becomes too hard. However, once you've encountered and dealt with difficult problems, you often find that you are more easily able to separate the different domains and contexts of the problems you face and then deal with each in turn. The bonus is that while you are on the road you are distinguishing between real problems and perceived problems. In my experience, the initial perception of a problem rarely matches reality.

In terms of initial decision making, it is very important to get people in a team working on aspects of how to solve issues as soon as the choice is made to go forward. In my experience, it is better to choose quickly and get it wrong than to make laborious decisions and spend time that you could be using to test your solution mired down in discussion, because those decisions will only be based on partial information and are therefore quite likely to be as flawed as a quick choice. The beauty of the quick, informed choice is that it can be reversed much more easily than a laboured decision because less emotion is invested in it. If you do learn that your choice is wrong, you can usually do something about it quickly. This way of doing things also lends itself to discovering simple, effective solutions rather than simplistic, ineffective solutions. While this type of decision making may require many iterations, ultimately the solutions they produce will be far more cost-effective because of their simplicity. An example of this would be the iPhone, which since its initial release has gone through multiple changes based on customer feedback, resulting in a more user friendly product.

Once everyone is working on the issues there is still much more to the task ahead. The next steps will be to quickly gather information about the problem and the timeframe necessary to resolve it, and to build a visual image of the problem and its resolution that is frequently updated and communicated to your team. In my experience, the use of mind maps, as well a preference for multiple one-on-one conversations rather than meetings and presentations, help to stay on top of what is going on as well as to be able to communicate the results to others. Mind maps are visual representations of thorough processes and plans, nowadays easily generated by one of a number of readily available online computer programs - my favourite being a site called mindmeister.com. These are helpful because, as a catalyst, you must be adept at tuning your messages so they are clearly understood and aligned with each participant.

Because it is unique individuals that make up a group, it is almost impossible to come up with one message that will resonate with everyone. Meetings are one venue in which to impart information and if you are a great speaker with lots of charisma, they may even close with people wanting to follow you. The problem arises in a situation where there are many specific actions to be undertaken, in which you need people to take personal responsibility for each piece. This is where the catalyst working one-on-one can make a very large contribution to the resolution of the toughest of challenges.

By using mind maps you can keep track of a large amount of information with a very simple and easy-to-remember method and you can quickly build a picture of where a process is becoming unbalanced. By communicating each task involved and the reason behind it to each team member working on implementing a solution, you are able to elicit a far more motivated response. With this means of communication, people often become enthusiastic about taking personal responsibility for their portion of the work, allowing you to step back from micro-managing and trust your employees to deliver positive results and to tell you when they run into a road block. Also, if the road block is another person in the organisation, you can approach them and find a resolution without anyone having to lose face, which also adds to the motivation. Little-by-little, as a catalyst you will be able to dissolve even the toughest Gordian knot in this way.

The Hunger Project tackles the Gordian knot of chronic hunger around the world using a workshop they call "vision commitment and action." With this simple tool, they have inspired women around the world to take control of the circumstances of their villages in environments in which people live on less than one dollar a day, where wealth is measured in grains of corn or rice and not coins.

Another issue that makes things more complex is peoples' propensity to use the word "but" both in acknowledging what we hear others say and in objecting to a course of action. I work hard to replace the word "but" with the word "and." "But" tends to be the delete button of progress, whereas "and" turns a "but" into a contribution. With the exception of direct quotations, this is the only place "but" is used in the entire book. So kick "but"; it's a bad habit! Remember, as a catalyst, it is important to always have a contingency plan, or three, in your back pocket, and - above all - keep an eye out for distinct issues that have been somehow scrambled together into a sticky mess.

A RECIPE FOR STONE SOUP

One generous portion of belief

One or more enthusiastic catalysts

One well defined context, communicated well

Testing for bad eggs so that you can leave them out

A heaping spoonful of emotion and trust

The ability to react proportionately and
level-headedly in times of crisis or change

A triple dose of reality

A preheated holistic present

A substantial dollop of perspective

A variety of questions including
self-questioning without self-doubt

Several spoonfuls of leadership
gravitas steeped in female energy

A large measure of inspiration fortified by deep listening

An embrace of change

A view of the bigger picture

Patience and presence

Effectual reasoning

Determination

An understanding that perception
is mutable and reality is not

Strategic insight

Personal and group goals created, shared and honoured

An embrace of the evolutionary
and iterative processes of change

Wheels Within Wheels

CHAPTER FIVE

Grassroots

*"For a community to be whole and
healthy, it must be based on people's
love and concern for each other."*
Millard Fuller

Ruby and John were very happy, living in the City and running their transport company together. The original employees were still working as woodworkers, polishers and builders, and they created light-weight, efficient vehicles that were used throughout the City and across the land to transport fruit, vegetables and other goods from near and far. The company had had to employ many other women and men and train them in the art of making carts and of driving them. It had taken a lot of organisation for Ruby to manage to draw up some rules of the road to make transport easier, such as requiring that everyone drive on the same side of the road. That made an enormous difference! The accident rate plummeted and everyone began to feel a great deal happier about entrusting themselves and their precious produce to the transport system. The neighbouring lands had agreed to adopt the same rules as well, which meant that it was now easier for everyone to travel here and there, and that was good for everybody. Ambitious as Ruby and John had been at the outset, they had never imagined just how far-reaching the effects of their company would be. Now, the streets were filled with quiet, organised vehicles that ran efficiently. The fruit-and-vegetable market overflowed with fresh produce and the company had begun to research the possibility of extending their service to even farther afield.

Across the border, in the convent, the nuns had had to break down their walls and extend their fields into the communal lands of the village, to keep up with the demand for their fine produce. Most of the townspeople were now employed in market gardening and they had started a new business of collecting refuse from the outskirts of the City and composting it to use as fertiliser on their fields. Attracted by the easier travel, some of the citizens of Ruby's homeland had begun to travel too, those who were patient enough to go though the lengthy application process. Ruby had seen a few familiar faces and had more contact with her old friends than she had had in several years. Her official exile had not been lifted, so she had not been home to see friends and family for a long time. However, sending letters was now easy. Before, there had been no effective postal system. Now, letters could be sent along with everything else. While there were times when Ruby felt nostalgic for her homeland, in general life was very good. Everything was good, in fact. As usual, of course, it could have been even better.

Ruby and John had had a son, whom they had called "Peter." Peter was a handsome, clever and kind child. They were both very proud of him and with good reason. They both devoted a great deal of time to teaching Peter everything they knew and to answering his many questions, which they wisely encouraged, as best they could.

Now that he was six, Peter was getting boisterous, and the apartment in which they lived seemed to have shrunk several sizes. Peter was fond of playing football and there was nowhere for him to kick his ball with his friends. He liked to get his hands dirty and the small apartment kitchen was not really the best spot for that.

"Maybe we should move out of the City," John said one evening as he ruefully surveyed the art with which Peter had decorated the kitchen wall when nobody was looking. "Peter needs some room to move around. This apartment isn't really great for a child. He should be able to kick a ball about. I didn't even notice that there was no garden when I moved in. Everything is different now that we have a child."

"Remember that we need to be near where we work," Ruby pointed out. "It won't be any fun for Peter if he only sees us at the weekends. Besides, our whole lives are in the City. This is where all our friends are. I really don't think that this is the right time for us to move."

"You are probably right. Yet this still isn't ideal. I used to love the City," John sighed. "And now it seems so built up. I remember that there used to be parks, long ago when I was a child. Now, those parks have been covered by apartment buildings and warehouses. Even the school where Peter goes doesn't have a playground. It's no good for a child. Somebody should really do something about it. I don't even know who to ask. Who is responsible for things like that?"

Ruby thought. She thought for a long time, and finally she had an idea. Every morning, when she walked Peter to school, they went past a vacant lot at the end of their block. The lot was surrounded by rusting wire and weeds and filled with rubbish. It was a real eyesore in what was generally quite an attractive neighbourhood. Still, despite the rubbish, Ruby had often seen song birds resting on the few trees that grew in the plot and some of the local cats on the ground beneath looking wistfully at the birds that they would never be able to catch. It seemed an awful shame for a vacant lot just to be left to fill up with debris when there were so many people who would appreciate having somewhere to play or just sit out-of-doors.

Hmm, Ruby thought. *I wonder if…*

Ruby had a friend in her apartment building. Her name was "Grace" and she was an elderly librarian at the City Hall. Grace was great: a wonderful friend and a constant inspiration to Ruby. She was always ready to sit and talk, and because she had a lot of time to read and a very non-stressful life, Grace had become hugely knowledgeable. Ruby had left school when she was still quite young and, while she had accumulated a great deal of experience and knew a lot about the world and how it worked, she was the first to admit that she was not widely read and that there was a great deal about which she knew almost nothing.

Grace showed her a new world, one far more diverse and exciting than anything Ruby had ever imagined. Despite the fact that she had always worked in the world of books and did not seem to engage much with many other people - and nor did she seem to have any particular interest in doing so - Grace was able to tell Ruby about the early explorers and the places, sights and cultures they had seen and the messages and learning that they had brought home from their travels around the world. She told her about philosophy and the many different types of political systems around the world. She told her about lands where the clothes, smells and sounds were utterly different to anything that Ruby had ever seen or even imagined. Ruby had always been proud of her ability to tell stories and now, in Grace, she had found another great storyteller. It was wonderful to relax and listen to her tales as Grace played with her little pet, a small albino mouse that ran up and down her arm and liked to perch on her shoulder, its small, intelligent eyes alert and its whiskers twitching as it watched and listened with every appearance of interest.

"There's one thing, Ruby," Grace said, "that all successful societies have in common, regardless of how different they may first seem."

"What's that?" Ruby asked.

"Where people are treated fairly, where they are not infantilised or repressed, where hard work is valued - these are the societies that are invariably both the wealthiest and the happiest."

Although Ruby had not travelled the world or read very widely, she thought about what she knew from her own life experiences and she agreed that what Grace was saying made perfect sense. It was almost uncanny how the Land from which Ruby came seemed to embody the exact opposite of what Grace was talking about.

In her younger days, Grace had travelled to many different lands and met many different philosophers. She had sat at the feet of some of the greatest thinkers in the world. Ruby had often asked Grace how she had lived in those days and what she had done. Grace had always answered her with nothing more than an enigmatic smile. She often told Ruby and, as he grew, Peter, stories about her travels and all that she had learned. She particularly loved to see how her stories were helping Peter grow into a bright, wide-eyed, curious child.

Grace had found in Ruby and her son what she had always wanted - someone to whom she could pass on her wisdom. While she had achieved much insight and activity, Grace had not been able to have children of her own and she keenly felt that loss.

In her quest, Ruby inquired of everyone she knew about the owner of the vacant lot; everyone just shook their heads and said that it had been empty for as long as they could remember. Long ago, before the area had been built up, it was just part of a field. Somehow, although nobody knew how or why, this particular plot had been left out of every building plan and had just been left to go to seed. Somebody must own it and yet nobody knew who. Grace said that she had been living in their apartment building ever since she left library school many years before and that she could not remember ever having seen it being used for anything. Once a year or so the City rat catcher came to unearth the rats that had made their nests inside and take them away and that was the only time anybody ever saw anyone going in or out.

Well, if nobody's using it, Ruby's great-grandmother whispered to her, *nobody will mind if someone borrows it.*

> *"It is in vain to say human beings ought to be satisfied with tranquillity: they must have action; and they will make it if they cannot find it."*
> **Charlotte Bronte, in Jane Eyre**

Ruby resolved to do something about the vacant lot herself. The very next day, she spoke to the parents of the children who went to school with Peter and to the other residents of her apartment building.

"I don't know," one person said. "It seems like an awful lot of work to have to do without even getting paid for it. Shouldn't the City be providing the park, anyway? Isn't that what we pay our taxes for?"

"I know," said Ruby. "The fact is, regardless of what the City is doing with our taxes, there just aren't any parks for the children to play in and most of the places where they could have been have been built upon. In any case the City doesn't seem to be very interested in parks at all. This is a chance to do something about it by ourselves. If it does work out, we'll all be repaid many times over, by having a beautiful, green space where our children can play. And that's not all. There are so many different types of people in this area and so few places for us all to meet, that I believe this park to be very important. As it is, the older boys are starting to get into fights in the street. If the children grew up playing together, they would be much less likely to see each other as strangers and enemies when they get old enough to start getting into fights."

"Won't it be dangerous, though?" another person asked. "Isn't there a risk of someone getting cut on the fence if we just let ourselves in without getting permission from the City authorities?"

Ruby smiled. She knew exactly what to do.

"Let's stop talking about the park for a little while," she said. "Let me tell you a story."

Everybody sat down and looked at Ruby expectantly and she began:

***

Long ago and far away, there was a place that was pretty close to being perfect, except for one thing. There was nowhere for the children to play and they had grown bored and listless. One day, as a group of parents waited at the school gate for their sons and daughters to come outside, they were approached by a curiously dressed man with a tiny albino mouse peering from his pocket.

"I'm organising a community picnic," the magician said (for that is what he was) and I would like to invite you and all your children for a delicious meal of Stone Soup..."

***

After they had heard the story, the mothers and fathers looked at each other with smiles of recognition and acknowledgement. Many of them had heard a version of the well-known story before and yet they all concurred that nobody had told it quite as well as this until now. Everyone agreed that there was a real need for a park in the area. Everyone had a child or knew a child who spent far too many sunny afternoons disconsolately gazing out the window instead of playing outside. Several of them had had to let out the waistbands of their rather chubby children's clothes and were concerned that they were not getting enough exercise. The story showed them that they really did have the means to make it happen and also that, if everyone did just a little, the work of maintaining the park would never be too onerous. Besides, they could all do with the exercise and it was nice to think of putting in an hour's work once or twice a week alongside their neighbours. The City was big and exhausting and it was too easy to find oneself always alone in the cocoon of one's own apartment to the detriment of all social life and sense of community.

So, one fine Sunday, they got to work. Some of the men brought wire clippers and cut an entry through the rusty wire that surrounded the lot. Ruby, Grace and other residents of the area donned overalls and heavy gloves and began the hard work of clearing out the rubbish and the tangled weeds. With her ready smile, Grace seemed to make everything easier: tangled undergrowth would, almost miraculously, come apart whenever she was in the area and apparently impenetrable rocks gave way easily to show the crumbly soil underneath. The soil was rich and loamy and when it was exposed to the sunlight, wild flowers began to germinate almost spontaneously, filling the space with flowers from one day to the next. The school started to compost the children's leftovers from lunch, which they were soon able to start adding to the topsoil that had been donated by a builder who had cleared it from the site of yet another apartment building.

When they saw what was happening, residents from the area were quick to offer seeds and bulbs. By the time a year had passed, Ruby and her friends had created a wonderful garden. There was a fruit-and-vegetable plot tended by the children themselves. The fruit and vegetables were harvested and used to fill their sandwiches for school. There was a rose-garden with a bench where old people could stop and rest on their way home from doing the shopping. There was an area that had been planted especially with heavily-scented plants - lavender and lilac and roses and mint - so that even those who could not see could enjoy the garden. There was a play area where swings and slides and games delighted all the children. There was a great big lawn that was just perfect for kicking a ball around on. In the trees, the song birds still perched and on the ground the cats still looked wistfully up. The garden had become the place where community news was exchanged, where the lonely could go, safe in the knowledge that they would meet someone to talk to and where no child, no matter how shy, was ever left without a playmate.

"You know," Ruby said to John one evening, "of all the work I have done over the years, I think this is the thing that makes me proudest."

Ruby looked out the window of their apartment. At the end of the block she could see their wonderful park, an oasis of green amid the tall, grey buildings of the city. The sound of children playing could be heard faintly in the distance.

The very next day, when Ruby took Peter to the park after school, it had been surrounded by high, impenetrable boarding and there was a large notice: "Health and safety warning: this park has not been passed for use." The signature at the bottom of the warning read: Thorald, City Manager.

Ruby's heart sank when she realised that the Bureaucrat-in-Chief's son had come to her adopted home and become the City Manager. This would spell disaster, she knew. There was a grave danger that Thorald would damage her business.

"First things first," Ruby resolved. "The park must be allowed to reopen."

Ruby knew that Thorald had a talent for seeming very sincere while at the same time acting without integrity. He had always been like that. She remembered how he had been elected to the school council years before, when they had both been young, by spreading malicious rumours about his opponent. This had obviously made him politically very successful – and at what cost? She had already seen how much her own Land had suffered as a result of his ideas and she dreaded to think of the havoc that he might be able to wreak on the City that she had made her home. Ruby wondered how Thorald was able to sleep at night, knowing what he did about himself. She decided that people like Thorald must simply be cut from a different cloth than the rest of humanity.

Ruby went to the City Hall and demanded a meeting with the authorities. She sat on one side of the big mahogany table and refused to leave until she had been given an explanation.

"This is not a real park," the authorities told her. "It is private property. It is not under the City jurisdiction. That means there's no insurance, so if one of the children falls off a swing and breaks their arm, they could sue us."

"The children have nowhere to play! There are no parks in this City!"

"Besides," the authorities continued, ignoring her, "as it is not an official park there is no way of regulating access. Anyone could go in! How can you be sure that a kidnapper won't go and take away one of the children? How would you feel then? It would all be your fault. And not just morally, either. You would also be personally and financially liable for anything that went wrong. "And…"

The door opened and a familiar figure walked into the room. He looked a little older and his hair had begun to recede a bit, yet it was the same Thorald who had picked off the legs of helpless money spiders when they had been in junior school together, and who, together with his father, had ruled for Ruby to be exiled from their homeland, many years before. He had put on a little weight and looked both smug and prosperous. Though Ruby did not like to admit it, she actually hated Thorald.

"Ruby," Thorald said with an unpleasant smile. "We meet again. I see that you are up to your old tricks. We cannot have that. People like you are dangerous."

Ruby drew herself up to her full height. "You cannot talk to me like that," she said. "I am not 'just' a humble citizen of your Land any more. I'm one of the biggest employers in the City. What is more, as you must surely realise, if it wasn't for my company, the Land would never have been able to attract tourists. Who do you think supplies the transportation for all the people who go to gape at your Palace? How do you think you, even you, would have come to the attention of the City Authorities if my transport company had not opened up the access to the Land?"

"Your little park is closing down, Ruby," Thorald said. "Get used to it. Your business is neither here nor there. Besides, if you hadn't done it, someone else would. You'll really have to stop thinking of yourself as someone special. Because you're not; you are just a jumped up girl from the lower classes who has no business going about telling other people what they should be doing with their lives."

Faced with Thorald's intransigence, there was little Ruby could do except tell the newspapers, so this is what she did, even as the children returned to playing alone, indoors. The story was covered on page eight and it seemed more than likely that the park was closed forever.

On the other side of town, a few days later, an old woman bought some fried potatoes wrapped in newspaper. She spread the potatoes out on the table and ate them and, as she did, a photograph caught her eye. She read the story that accompanied it with gathering interest. The story read and the potatoes eaten, the old woman put on her coat and made her way as quickly as she could (which was not very quickly, as her old, tired legs had had very little exercise in recent years) to Ruby and John's factory where she rushed past the surprised receptionist and into Ruby's office, brandishing her piece of newspaper.

"That land is mine," she said. "All mine. And I don't need it. If you promise to keep it as a park, and never to close it again, I will sign it over to you and I will put some money towards an annuity to cover the insurance."

The very next day, the boarding came down and the children were soon back at play.

"You know," Ruby said to her new friend. "Thorald did make one good point. It might not be a bad idea to have an adult around when the children are playing, just to keep an eye on things. Some of the bigger ones do get a little boisterous at times."

"Well," the old woman said. "I would be happy to come every afternoon after school and spend some time here. I'm certainly very bored with sitting at home and crocheting doilies. I have more doilies than I could use in a lifetime. I even make the cat wear one on his head, just to give it some use and he hates that..."

From then on, the play area had an attendant. The children loved the old woman and, for her part, she was delighted when they started calling her "Granny."

One day, one of the children, a small girl with long dark hair and a shy smile, came in quietly and played by herself, watching the other girls and boys and politely resisting their attempts to engage her in their games. This little girl lived on the other side of town and under ordinary circumstances she would never even have heard of the park. Earlier that day, however, the strangest thing had happened: While she had been looking at a book in the City Library, a note, handwritten on lavender-scented paper, had popped out from between the pages. On the note there was a carefully drawn map to the park with the suggestion that she should go and take a look for herself. Most curious of all was the fact that the note had been addressed to the little girl in person. She had looked around to see if anyone was playing a trick on her, yet there was nobody there except the librarian, who seemed to be very busy behind her desk with a large box of indexing cards.

The little girl's name was Orna and she was Thorald's daughter. Orna's mother had left when she was just a baby and she had never returned, so Orna was a very lonely little girl indeed. Her father loved her very deeply, and he was also a very busy man, so Orna spent most of her time by herself. Orna was very happy that, at long last, she had a park to play in and she loved to watch the other children play, although she did not dare accept their invitations to friendship, for fear of what her father would say if he ever found out.

Life was good. Ruby and John continued to prosper and Peter continued to grow and to pass his days happily, studying and learning with his peers and playing in the park. His greatest dream, which gave his parents immense pleasure, was that one day, when he was older, he would go to work with them in the factory.

Lessons from Grassroots

In my experience, life works best when you have integrity. Indeed the more you integrity you have, i.e. the more you are true to what you say, the more life works for the better. I see business as part of a balanced life, not distinct from it, and therefore integrity in your business is also essential to its performance. Erhart, et. al.[11] argue that operating with integrity in business is not just the right thing to do, it is also a better way to work in terms of creating a successful viable business while also empowering people and enhancing their quality of life. They go so far as to describe it as "the platform for superior leadership, a guaranteed opportunity for maximum performance, an important Factor of Production," and as a way to realise "the power potentially available in Morality."

They define integrity as "the objective state or condition of an object, system, person, group, or organisational entity," and "the state or condition of being whole, complete, unbroken, sound, perfect." They go on to say that, "Integrity does determine workability, and workability determines the available opportunity for performance. No matter about the other factors, one cannot perform beyond the available opportunity for performance, and that is determined by Integrity. Thus, Integrity is an important Factor of Production;" in other words, the more integrity you have in the various areas of your life, the more things you have completed, the more you will be able to achieve.

Integrity, in my opinion, is also the foundation of personal empowerment. I subscribe to the ideal that

---

[11] 2007.

integrity is simply honouring your word such that you either keep it or, if you know you cannot keep it, you clear the situation with whomever you have given your word to such that they are still satisfied. Thus, for me the basis of empowerment is having the ability to give your word to something and then honour the word you gave. Anything that gets in the way of that, either externally or internally, is disempowering. A little disempowerment, a little break in integrity, can go a long way towards disrupting your whole life, especially in the complex world of today. Something distracting you at the wrong moment can wreak havoc, so it pays to look after your integrity – to complete the things you have not completed and to honour your word.

Anyone who wants to succeed in business or in life needs to understand that generosity and sharing are an immensely important aspect of success. Real entrepreneurs know that what is good for their community is more than likely to be good for them, as well. Understanding the importance of generosity helps us to be more open, in every way: more open to give, more open to the lessons that the world offers, and more open to possibility.

A RECIPE FOR STONE SOUP

One generous portion of belief

One or more enthusiastic catalysts

One well defined context, communicated well

Testing for bad eggs so that you can leave them out

A heaping spoonful of emotion and trust

The ability to react proportionately and
level-headedly in times of crisis or change

A triple dose of reality

A preheated holistic present

A substantial dollop of perspective

A variety of questions including
self-questioning without self-doubt

Several spoonfuls of leadership
gravitas steeped in female energy

A large measure of inspiration fortified by deep listening

An embrace of change

A view of the bigger picture

Patience and presence

Effectual reasoning

Determination

An understanding that perception
is mutable and reality is not

Strategic insight

Personal and group goals created, shared and honoured

An embrace of the evolutionary
and iterative processes of change

Integrity

Grassroots

CHAPTER SIX

A Challenge Too Far

Time passed, as it tends to do. The years were full: full of work and play, full of seeing Peter grow into manhood and of seeing the City in which they lived grow and prosper, despite the tightening web of rules and regulations that were put in place by Thorald, the City Manager.

Ruby and John were now middle-aged. There were days when they bemoaned their grey hairs and the wrinkles that were now evident at the corners of their eyes, though generally, life was still very good and they felt just as young and vigorous as they ever had. Their son Peter had grown into a fine young man, who now worked with them in the company. At twenty-five, he looked just as John had at that age - just a lot less cross. Peter was still a source of tremendous pride and joy to his parents, both of whom secretly hoped that he would find a mate soon, settle down and have a family so that they could become grandparents while they were still quite young.

Ruby and John had recently celebrated their fiftieth birthdays - they had been born within a week or two of each other. The joint party had been held in their local park, with many of their friends. Grace had brought the cake and although she must have been quite old - she had never revealed her exact age - she seemed to have just as much energy as ever. Despite the fact that Thorald was still the City Manager, he had not been able to rule the City with the same iron fist that his father used back in the Land, so spontaneous events were still possible. Gradually, however, a creeping tendency towards state regulation had come to characterise much of the City's culture. Ruby and John resisted it as best they could and as one of the largest employers in the City and as a company that was known for treating its workers fairly, they were largely immune from the worst of it.

Even Thorald did not want to risk damaging a big company, especially one that provided the transport to the tourists who visited his father's jurisdiction. They had all got in the habit of just avoiding each other, a habit that was not hard to maintain as they moved in very different circles. Thorald was middle-aged, too. He had never found another companion following the disappearance of his wife and even his strongest detractors could see that he must be a very lonely man. He lived with his daughter, Orna, who worked for him in the City Council. She was the apple of his eye and it was his fondest hope that she would eventually take over his position.

In the factory, things were going well. John was doing an excellent job of maintaining control of the raw materials that were used to create the carts. Every day, he went down to the port to meet the supplier who brought the woods and other material from far and wide. Peter often accompanied him. They both loved the fresh, cold air that blew in from the sea and they loved to meet the sailors, who always had remarkable tales to tell about how things were done in other countries. Just like his father, Peter had always been too busy to travel much. He hoped to be able to change this, as he longed to see the rest of the world and especially the Land from whence his mother had come.

John often reminisced about when he had been a child. In those days, the girls and boys of the City had flocked to the port to swim. They had loved the feeling of the cool, clean water on their young bodies. Often, in their exuberance, they had rushed to the port straight after school and hurled themselves into the water to swim, leaving their clothing behind them on the beach. John was sorry that Peter had never had this experience, as swimming had been banned ever since Thorald had become the City Manager.

"Well, Dad," Peter said now, as he turned to face his father. "I'm no fan of Thorald and yet I have to admit that maybe, in this case, he has a point. Swimming is dangerous; in some other countries, people drown all the time. I think he's probably right in this case. You can't drown if you don't get into the water in the first place."

"You can't believe everything you read, Peter," John retorted. "I know that I would rather know how to swim than not if I found myself on a sinking ship."

As they debated, one of the ships prepared to leave. The sailors hoisted the sails and started to wind up the clockwork propellers. Slowly and majestically, the ship left the wharf and set out across the water. However, no one realised that something had been forgotten.

The heavy rope that had held the ship fast to the wharf had not been loaded on board and now, treacherously and unseen, it snaked its way around Peter's ankle, pulling him into the water. John called out in alarm as Peter sank beneath the dark water. Such was the noise of the engines of the shop that the sailors did not hear him. John could see Peter's body being pulled along under the water. He knew that Peter could not swim and that he had only moments to save him. John did not have a moment to waste.

Tearing off his shoes, John leapt into the water and struck out as fast as he could, swimming towards the departing ship. He was fully clothed and the water dragged heavily at his legs and arms. He was nearly there. He could see Peter's wide-eyed face underneath the green water, and his pale hands, opening and closing just as helplessly as they had when he had been a newborn.

A burst of pain blossomed in John's chest, eliminating all other experience and banishing conscious thought. He looked towards Peter and saw that his eyes were closed and then saw two lean, brown arms quickly and deftly untangling the rope around his legs and then pull Peter's head from beneath the water. John closed his eyes and welcomed the cold embrace of the sea. Slowly, he sank beneath the water. The light receded behind him and soon he was gone completely.

The messenger who rushed to the factory brought Ruby both the good and the terrible news: John, the partner of her life and the man whom she loved, was dead, yet Peter, who had nearly gone too, had been saved. A mysterious swimmer, clad from head to toe in a black, figure-hugging swimming costume, had pulled him from the Port, emptied his lungs of the sea-water that had almost killed him and then slipped away, leaving him in the care of the crowd that had gathered to help. Nobody knew the identity of Peter's saviour.

Ruby was devastated. For the first weeks after her loss, she concentrated all her efforts on making Peter well again. John's funeral came and went. She attended it stoically, without even tears in her eyes. Afterwards, she could barely remember it; it seemed to have passed as if in a dream. She could remember Grace standing beside her at the graveside, her arm firmly around Ruby's shoulders. Afterwards, Grace had prepared her a tisane and had made her drink it and go to bed, where she had slept for twenty-four hours.

As Peter recovered, Ruby's heart filled with grief and tears flowed uncontrollably from her eyes. She felt sure that John would never have died had it not been for the City Manager's absurd rules against swimming. Without those rules, Peter would have been able to swim to safety by himself. It was all Thorald's fault! Her helplessness in the face of the awful events that had taken place caused her to doubt everything further. What was the point of working so hard for her business and her community when other people's rules and regulations and attitude could break down all that she built? What was the point of anything? Maybe she should just have stayed at home in her Land and put up with things the way they were, accepting that she was just one person and that there was nothing she could do to change the world. Maybe she had been wasting her time her whole life.

As Peter grew stronger and stronger, Ruby sank into a deep, apparently immovable depression. She stopped brushing her hair and taking her daily showers. She ate barely enough to keep body and soul together. She began to look much, much older than her still-youthful fifty years. She ceased to be someone fully alive and became a woman who was waiting for death. There seemed to be nothing that anyone could do to help her escape from this fog of misery. She was utterly at the mercy of her own emotions. Refusing to accept them and embrace them for what they were, she had no way of overcoming them.

Peter was desperately worried about his mother and he was also racked with guilt because of the fact that his accident had led to his father's death. If only he had been more careful, he thought, none of this would have happened. Despite these feelings of culpability, Peter was very thankful that he had been saved; less for himself than for his mother, who would surely have ended her own life if she had not had someone to live for. He decided that he would have to help Ruby out of this morass of despair, come what may.

First, he tried to cajole her. This was useless. In response to her requests to please come to the workshop and see what the workers were doing, Ruby would just go to her room, get into bed and turn her face to the wall. Then, he tried to bully her by shouting about her responsibilities at the factory. This did not work either and it was almost more than he could bear to see the tears running down her face, clear as crystals. Then, Peter tried to be resolutely cheerful and avoided all mention of his father and his death, talking brightly about what was going on at work and in the City as though nothing bad had ever happened. This approach was similarly useless. Without any more ideas as to how he could help his mother to get on with her life, Peter stopped trying for the moment.

Peter often wondered about the identity of the swimmer who had pulled him from the water. Only someone young would have been able to swim so strongly and confidently, he thought, and yet swimming had been banned in the City for over twenty years and no children had been allowed so much as to dip a toe into the water, so who could it have been? He thought that he remembered catching a glimpse of an olive-skinned face, and large, nearly luminous, dark eyes before the mysterious swimmer disappeared, yet he was not sure. The question haunted him and, often, he woke at night having dreamt about the swimmer. Still, he did not know who it was, although he was almost sure that the slight figure had been that of a woman. Every night, he dreamed of the moment when he had been saved; he always woke just before he saw her face.

Because of Ruby's terrible depression, Peter had had to take over most of her daily responsibilities at the factory, leaving him little time to deal with his own grief or with his growing obsession with finding out the identity of the person who had saved him. Ruby had usually been the one to deal with City Hall and the many permissions that had to be obtained, and now Peter did it. While these tasks were exceptionally tedious, he was thankful for them now, as at least they meant that he had something specific to do every day and did not dwell all the time on his father's death and his own significant, if accidental, role in it.

One day, Peter was queuing for his Wheelage Permit A41 when he saw the young woman working behind the counter. She was not very tall and she was very slight, yet the tautness of her body suggested great strength and her determined chin hinted at her strong personality. Her dark brown hair was tied back in a knot behind neat, small ears, each of which sported a small pearl earring. She had an olive complexion and great, dark, wide-set eyes. She struck a chord of recognition in him immediately. He could not fathom it until their eyes met and she brushed away a lock of her hair with a suddenly familiar hand; the hand that had saved his life.

Peter's heart raced as he realised that he had just identified the person who had saved him. He wanted to thank her and yet he knew that he could not say a word: swimming had been banned in the City since his childhood and he could get her into terrible trouble!

When he approached the desk, the young woman looked up again from her paperwork. She flushed and looked back down to avoid his gaze. She seemed to be attempting to will him not to speak. What was going on?

Peter pushed his application form across the desk: "I need a Wheelage Permit A41," he said with all the emotion he could muster. He gazed into her eyes and tried to express some of what he was feeling.

"You'll have to come back with that signed and stamped in triplicate," she said. She pushed the piece of paper back across the desk towards him. Their hands touched. For each, it was as if a current of electricity passed between them.

"On second thoughts," she said. "There is an escape clause that's covered in the bylaws 765-7. As today is the first Monday of the month, we don't really need that in triplicate. Don't worry. I'll make sure you get your Wheelage Permit A41."

"Thank you."

Peter waited outside the office after working hours and, when Orna emerged, he approached her.

"I know who you are," he said in a low voice. "You are the person who pulled me from the water and saved my life. I owe you everything. How can I thank you?"

"Yes," she said quietly. "I know who you are too. You were always too busy playing in the park to look at me, the quiet little girl who kept to herself. I used to watch you every day and see how confident and happy you were, playing with your friends on the grass. How I wanted to join in your games, and yet I never did, because I was afraid. I knew that my father would never have allowed me to play with someone like you. He would have been angry, had he known that I had taken to visiting the park. I never thought that, years later, we would meet again. And yet I recognised you the moment I saw you standing there beside the ocean with your father."

Peter took Orna's hand and they walked together through the City where they had both grown up and, as if they could read each other's minds, straight towards the port where Peter had nearly drowned. They spoke easily, as if they had known each other all their lives. Indeed, this was how they both felt. Orna told him about how she had grown up as the daughter of Thorald, the City Manager.

"He is not a bad man," she said. "Not really. He does love the City and his job. It's just that he has never been able to see things from anyone else's point of view. It's a common failing in our family. My grandfather, you see, is the Bureaucrat-in-Chief in a Land some distance from here…"

Peter told Orna all he knew about his mother's childhood and they realised that they had a great deal in common; both of them were descended from parents who had come from the Land, and their families had been strangely bound together ever since Ruby had been sent into exile.

Orna told Peter how, ever since childhood, she had loved to swim. It had started when she used to sneak away from her home and go down the port. She would lie face down on the wooden boardwalk and watch the fish underneath, darting in the water. How she loved to see their silver-hued, streamlined bodies moving quickly through the cold water! She envied them the freedom they seemed to have. She envied them their cold-blooded indifference. She had always resented her own turbulent emotions, as they seemed to hold her back and stop her from being content with her place in life. Even as a child, Orna had always longed for everything to be different.

She did not know exactly what she wanted; just that it was not this. Orna loved her father very much and she knew that he loved her, too. It was just that he was so busy. He almost never had time to see her and he had always refused to speak to her about her mother and why she had left them all those years before. Orna wished that she did not care and yet she did and she was sure that she always would.

One day, Orna had met an older woman who had been strolling on the boardwalk when she went down for her customary walk. With her proud expression and the thick white hair pulled into a bun at the nape of her neck, she looked quite familiar, although Orna could not pinpoint exactly why.

"They are beautiful, aren't they?" the woman had said, nodding towards the fish. "I bet you'd like to swim, too. There's nothing to beat the feeling of the water against your skin."

"More than anything in the world!" Orna had confided. "I know I mustn't though. It is against the rules and my Daddy is the City Manager, so I will never learn how to swim."

"We don't always have to follow the rules, you know," the woman said. "Sometimes rules are silly and when we are really sure that the rule is silly and that we are not going to hurt anybody by breaking it we can make up our own minds. If you like, I will teach you how to swim. I'm not as young as I once was, yet I have always been a very strong swimmer and I break the rules about swimming every day! It is true that swimming can be dangerous. However, if you know how to take care, you will be able to keep yourself very safe. If you are interested, I will teach you about tides and winds and the ways of the water and I can help you be a wonderfully strong and confident swimmer. Only if you really want it, of course."

"Really?"

"Really."

The woman, whose name was "Grace," had spent years teaching Orna how to swim as gracefully as a salmon and with the strength of a killer whale. They swam early in the morning and late at night when the full moon provided them with enough illumination to see where they were going and when there was nobody about to see that they were flouting one of the most often-repeated rules of the City. Grace never told Orna where she lived, what she did, or why she was going to so much trouble to teach the girl how to swim and, quite quickly, Orna learned not to ask Grace too many questions, as these were always answered with an enigmatic smile and nothing more. Even after she noticed Grace in the library one day, somehow Orna knew that Library Grace was not to be confused with Aquatic Grace.

Although he was still grieving for his father, Peter was in love. Being so happy to have found the love of his life, he wanted more than anything for his mother to share his joy and welcome Orna into the family. It seemed to him that it must be much more than coincidence that the woman who had taught Orna to swim was none other than his mother's close friend, Grace, and that the person to have saved him from drowning none other than Orna, the granddaughter of the very man who had sent his mother into exile from their Land, so many years ago.

"I am sure that, together, we can do something to heal the rift between our families," Peter said to Orna, "and to show Thorald and maybe even your grandfather, that there really is no need for them to be so scared of everything that they feel the need to ban most things…"

Fate had thrown yet another obstacle in the lovers' path. Growing suspicious of his daughter's lengthy absences from her home, Thorald had had her followed and had been horrified to learn that the object of her devotion was none other than Peter, the only son of the woman whom he both hated and feared more than anyone else in the world, because she represented everything that he found terrifying and strange.

When Thorald turned up at the factory, Peter was sure that it was going to be difficult, and he was right.

"I don't want you seeing my daughter," Thorald said bluntly. "You are no good for her. She is not for you. We are not the same type of person, you and I. I have arranged for Orna to be accompanied everywhere by five bodyguards, all of whom are under strict instructions to have you locked up if you so much as dare to speak to her. Orna is very busy at work now and I'm going to ensure that she focuses on her career from now on so that she can take over my work, when the time comes. From this day forth, Orna will not have any time to spend with the likes of you."

"What?" Peter cried. "Will you never let me see her? I love her so much! Are you a monster?"

Thorald smiled unpleasantly. "Tell you what, to prove I am no monster," Thorald said, "if you think that you are so great, you can see her when she manages to reduce her workload from ten hours a day to one, without compromising the quality of her work in any way."

"Thank you," Peter said. "You have given me hope."

"Pah!" said Thorald, "Not really. You'll never manage to do that. In fact, you'll be doing yourself a favour if you just give up now and stop thinking about my little girl."

Peter went home and thought long and hard about the work that Orna had to do. It was mostly repetitive, bureaucratic work that called for the filling in of many forms in triplicate and the filing of all the forms in the appropriate folder. How he wished that there were some sort of a machine to do the work! Nothing of the sort existed, however. He toyed with the idea of inventing a sort of pen that could write on three forms at once. Anything that he was able to cobble together was far too unwieldy for Orna to use. He stayed up until long into the night for many nights in a row, finding that all his ideas were useless and that there seemed to be no answer in sight.

Peter realised that there was only one person who could help him now: Ruby. More than anyone he knew, Ruby was able to look beyond obstacles and find solutions that nobody else had been able to imagine before. And yet she was still desperately depressed; barely managing to get up in the morning. Ruby had continued not to eat enough and had grown gaunt and pale. How on earth was Peter going to be able to persuade her to help him, when she was not even able to help herself?

Peter went to his mother's apartment where she was spending this day, like so many, with her face pressed against the glass, staring unblinkingly across the City towards the port that had claimed her husband's life.

"Mum," Peter whispered to her, taking her hand. "I have found the woman that I love and I need your help to make her mine."

Ruby looked at him with hollow eyes. "My son," she said. "There is nothing I can do for you. There is nothing any of us can do. The City Manager has destroyed everything. There is nothing here for me anymore. I am just waiting to die; if I had the courage, I would end my life by my own hand."

Peter took a deep breath.

"Mum," he said. "Let me tell you a story." He led Ruby away from the window and sat her down and then he began:

***

Once upon a time, an old dowager's sorrow had sucked all the joy from the village she owned nearly completely and left the villagers hungry and desperate. A magician came and, finding no joy or food to be had, prepared a soup of boiled stone which he encouraged the villagers to join him in brewing and feasting on. Each of the inhabitants of the village contributed an ingredient or two and, when the soup was done, it was quite delicious. Nonetheless, everyone agreed that it still seemed to lack a certain something. When all the village had gathered together, the magician noticed that one house remained closed; that of the dowager. The magician proclaimed that the magic stone could not work unless the entire village participated. He convinced all the villagers to do whatever they could to persuade the dowager to join in.

After much argument, the villagers began to remember the times before the woman had been widowed and the kindness that had dwelt in her heart. Each contributed a token or a kind word and gave them all to the magician, who sent a young boy to see the dowager with the gifts. She was so moved by the combined efforts of her people that she came to the feast with the pinch of salt that was all that the soup had required to make it the most delicious it could be. She never looked back. Although she never forgot her love, she began to live again…

***

When he had finished the story, Peter unwrapped a small parcel of notes and trinkets that all the people who loved Ruby had given him to let her know how much they cared. There were gifts from the adults whose childhoods had been brightened by the park in which they had spent so many happy hours, from the children who still played there, from a new generation of nuns, who continued to send their produce to market and from many of the employees at the factory, which was one of the biggest and most successful companies in the City.

Ruby looked at him properly for the first time in months and saw much of John in Peter's steady gaze as the wisdom in his story resonated with her.

As the scales fell from her eyes, Ruby finally saw her sorrow for what it was - a guest whom she had been refusing to acknowledge. Something that she had been fighting against when she should have accepted it and held it as the signifier for her deep love for John rather than a burden to be pushed away and rejected.

Ruby looked at Peter with tears in her eyes.

"I will help you," she said. "Of course, my child, I will help in any way that I can."

"Nothing can stop the man with the right mental attitude from achieving his goal; nothing on earth can help the man with the wrong mental attitude."
Thomas Jefferson

Meanwhile, Thorald had made Orna's work much more challenging than before, rendering Peter's task all the more difficult. Thorald had put Orna in charge of a duty that was probably the most difficult in the whole City.

The City had grown enormously in recent years - in large part, because of the improved transport and infrastructure that had resulted from all of John and

Ruby's efforts. It was continuing to grow and keeping it clean was a constant struggle. The litter and rubbish that blew here and there on windy days was a telling symptom of the problem. It was not as though the City authorities were not trying to deal with the situation. Quite the reverse, in fact. Every day, thousands of workers came and took away all the rubbish, bearing it off in their hand-carts to great dumps on the outskirts of town where scavengers took away anything that was remotely useful and piled the rest up to be picked over by seagulls and rats. There was a huge amount of coordination to take care of and the rubbish was so vast in quantity that it was becoming increasingly difficult to deal with, as well as the associated issues of sanitation and health.

Together, Ruby and Peter considered the situation at great length.

"You know," Peter said after several weeks of careful deliberation. "We could eliminate clothing and paper from the rubbish completely if I set up a business that collected these items separately and used them to make new paper and cloth for sail-boats and long-distance sail-carts. As it is, we have to buy the cloth from overseas and it has always been one of our biggest expenses. We might be able to achieve several things at once..."

"True," said Ruby. "And although nobody really likes to talk about it all that night soil that gets carted away every morning would be a fantastic element in the municipal composting system that we could start up."

Six months later, Peter's new businesses were taking away so much of the rubbish that most of the waste deployment workers were now working for him and Orna had much less to do.

Triumphantly, Peter presented himself to Thorald.

"I have done what you asked. Won't you let me see her now?"

"Certainly not!" Thorald said. "You might think that you are clever. I know, however, that you will never be able to deal with the next part of your challenge. I have put Orna in charge of the Schools Department now. We have the biggest drop-out rate in the entire region. You must have seen for yourself all the teenagers hanging about the streets and getting up to mischief. They are the ones who grow up to be the unemployable adults who end up in the stocks or in jail. If you manage to fix that situation for her, you can see her."

Thorald laughed and yet his laughter was somehow hollow. He felt secure in his assumption that Peter would not be able to win this time yet, truth be told, the problem of the hoards of uneducated boys and girls thronging the City had been exercising his mind for some time, because they were both a drain on the City's resources and an aesthetic carbuncle on the face of the town that he had, almost despite himself, grown to love.

Peter went home. He had liked school and had always been in the A-stream, thanks in large part to the great support provided to him by his parents. Even then, although they had rarely met, he had been dimly aware that there were plenty of girls and boys who seemed to hate to learn and who left school early. While some went into good jobs and did well, it was undeniable that some grew into the sort of adults one would cross the road to avoid. Peter could see that there was a problem and yet he had no idea how he could start to address it. Nor did Ruby.

"Don't give up hope," Ruby said. "Even if we do not know very much about education, we do know someone who is very knowledgeable about the field. Grace will be able to help."

Grace listened to the problem with a smile.

"I think the biggest problem here," she said. "Is that people assume that all learning has to do with books and reading and writing, and that people who are not good at these things are simply stupid. If we start with the assumption that these girls and boys are not stupid, we have already made progress. Instead of focusing on the problem of their unruly behaviour on the streets, what we need to do is find out what they are good at and what they like to do, and then teach them those things first. People who are doing work that they like and that they can do competently are much less likely to cause any trouble to themselves or others."

On Grace's suggestion, Peter started a vocational school adjacent to the factory. The young people were taught how to make carts and drive them, how to sort timber and other materials and how to deal with customers. They were shown how it was important to know the basics of reading and writing to work well, and most of them agreed that it was worth putting up with a little book-learning in exchange for having the opportunity to earn their own money and the respect of their families and friends. Many of them showed every sign of becoming excellent employees in the years to come and more than one or two seemed to have great leadership potential.

Peter went to Thorald, armed with his latest success and hopeful that, at last, he would be allowed to see his love. His nights were filled with dreams of her and his days had no meaning beyond doing all he could to accomplish the tasks that her father insisted were necessary before they could be together.

"I have done everything you asked," Peter said. "And I am very grateful to you. Our family was one of the biggest employers in the City before and yet now we are more successful than ever. And it is all thanks to you and your useful suggestion that I see what I could do about all the young people on the streets. So now can I see Orna? I think that I have more than demonstrated how strongly I feel about her."

Thorald was absolutely furious. He had never expected that Peter would be able to achieve all he had done, and so quickly, too. Even more, he had never imagined that the difficult tasks he was setting the young man would lead to his increased success. This was an outrage!

"Sure," Thorald said with a wild glint of desperation in his eye. "Of course you can see her. When she has finished her new job, that is. I have put Orna in charge of removing all the beggars from the streets of the City, so when every single one of those wastrels is in secure employment, you can see her. And don't hold your breath. The poor, you know, are always with us."

With some bravado Peter took on this challenge on the condition that it would be the last and Thorald, despite his reservations, was still cocky enough to agree to this.

Despondent, Peter went home and told Ruby about the new task that he had been set. He was very surprised when Ruby smiled. He had not seen her smile so broadly for a very long time.

"Ha!" Ruby said. "Thorald doesn't know who he is dealing with here! For years I have wanted to do something for the beggars and only now has he given me the opportunity."

"What's that?"

"Well," Ruby said. "Now that we are composting all the City's night soil and food waste, we have a very pressing need for gardeners…"

Ruby and Peter gave all of the beggars inspiration and productive work to do. Some were mad and had delusions and they gave them work that they were able to manage. Many found that their delusions diminished with their new responsibilities. Some were women and men down on their luck and were more than happy to have secure employment for the first time in years. The story of Ruby's own time as a mendicant, when she had been forced to present herself to the convent and beg for mercy, gave them something to relate to, as she never let them feel condescended to. They worked very hard in their new jobs and were rewarded with good pay and safe working conditions. A few of the beggars, however, were genuine wastrels or really incapable and it seemed to be nigh on impossible to make them into models of industry.

"There's not a great deal we can do with them," Ruby confided to Peter. "So we'll put them all in white coats and call them 'inspectors'. At least that will keep them busy and out of trouble!"

For years, Ruby had been buying up vacant plots all over the City, small and large. She had always planned to turn these into parks and gardens. This had never been possible before. Now, thanks to all the compost that Peter's new waste management company was creating, flowers grew where before there was nothing other than cracked concrete.

Once again, Peter made his way to see Thorald. He found him sitting slouched in his fine, leather-upholstered chair.

"Sir," he said. "With all due respect, I have done what you asked. I have taken the beggars off the streets and given them all employment. Orna really can't have very much to do in the Beggaring Department."

"I give up," Thorald said. "You have worn me down. You can see Orna. She wants to marry you, you know, and has been working me over every day to get me to back down. I can only hope that you are worthy of her, although I sincerely doubt it. I love her so much and it is hard for me to believe that you will treat her even half as well as she deserves."

Then Peter did something that Thorald could never have predicted. He threw his arms around the older man in a bear hug and kissed him warmly on the cheek.

"I know that things have been difficult between us," he said, understating the case considerably. "We are family now...Dad. And I am sure that we are going to find a way to become close and even grow to be good friends. I will make that my mission. I have always been told that a daughter's love of her father is a sacred thing, and I want you to know that I would never come between you."

Lessons from A Challenge Too Far

In his book *The Talent Code*, author Daniel Coyle makes the important point that innate talent is the least important element in success. What is much more important, he explains, is dedicated practice and learning. According to Coyle, the brains of growing children can actually be shaped by practicing skills and these changes are much more important than any so-called "innate" talent or ability that they might have. Simply put, the more we practice a skill, whatever it may be, the more quickly and efficiently our brain is able to perform tasks: "Repetitive use of connections in the brain, or practice, triggers cells called oligodendrocytes, which wrap layer upon layer of myelin around these connections. This optimises the connections, which makes them more like a broadband Internet connection than a dial-up.[12]" So while many great leaders may be born with skills that allow them to lead, many more can become great leaders through practice and persistence.

---

[12] Coyle, 2009.

A Recipe for Stone Soup

One generous portion of belief

One or more enthusiastic catalysts

One well defined context, communicated well

Testing for bad eggs so that you can leave them out

A heaping spoonful of emotion and trust

The ability to react proportionately and
level-headedly in times of crisis or change

A triple dose of reality

A preheated holistic present

A substantial dollop of perspective

A variety of questions including
self-questioning without self-doubt

Several spoonfuls of leadership
gravitas steeped in female energy

A large measure of inspiration fortified by deep listening

An embrace of change

A view of the bigger picture

Patience and presence

Effectual reasoning

Determination

An understanding that perception
is mutable and reality is not

Strategic insight

Personal and group goals created, shared and honoured

An embrace of the evolutionary
and iterative processes of change

Integrity

Disciplined, diligent practice

A Challenge Too Far

CHAPTER SEVEN

The Circle Closes

*"History says, Don't hope
on this side of the grave.
But then, once in a lifetime
the longed for tidal wave
of justice can rise up,
and hope and history rhyme."*
Seamus Heaney

Shortly after Peter and Orna's engagement party, which was held in the factory and attended by all their good friends and even Thorald, who managed to be quite pleasant for the evening, Ruby received a missive from her homeland, delivered by one of her own cart drivers.

"Dear Ruby," the letter read. "It is with great pleasure that I revoke your exile and invite you back to the Land that you left so many years ago. And now that my granddaughter and your son are about to be united in matrimony, perhaps you can travel home and we can plan the festivities together. I am sure that we have a lot to talk about."

The letter had been signed by none other than the Bureaucrat-in-Chief.

Ruby showed the letter to Grace.

"What do you think?" she asked. "Can I trust him? Can I forgive and forget? I have hated this man all my life. I don't mind about him being Orna's grandfather, honestly I don't. She's a delightful young woman. That doesn't stop me hating him, though. What do you think I should do?"

Grace looked at Ruby. A little smile played on her lips.

"It is certainly true," Grace said. "That the Bureaucrat-in-Chief has done many terrible things and that you have more than one reason to hate him. And yet, in a strange way, those very same terrible things have also enabled you to become the person you are today. What would have become of you if you had stayed in the Land? What would you gain by continuing to hold on to your hatred and suffering?"

"In reality, serendipity accounts for one percent of the blessings we receive in life, work and love. The other 99 percent is due to our efforts."
Peter McWilliams

Ruby thought about what Grace said and had to concede that she had made a very good point.

"All right," she said. "I'll go and you must come with me. I don't have the courage to face that particular trip on my own."

Grace smiled her enigmatic smile. "Believe me," she said. "I have my own reasons for going there, too. I will explain when I get there. For now, suffice to say that I too left that particular Land under a cloud."

Ruby looked sharply at Grace. She had never asked her anything about her past, sensing that Grace did not want to talk about it. This was the very first time that she had heard anything about Grace being from the same Land as herself and she was very eager to hear more about this surprising revelation. Grace had already moved on to something else and Ruby knew better than to try and make her talk about a subject that was so evidently closed. She hoped that they would be able to revisit it very soon.

*"What I cannot recreate
I do not understand."*
Richard Feynman

The Bureaucrat-in-Chief was a very old man. He had seen more than a hundred summers light the fields and more than a hundred winters spread their mantle of white across the Land. At first, when he had heard that his beloved granddaughter Orna was about to marry the son of the woman whom he had sent into exile more than a quarter-century before, the Bureaucrat-in-Chief had been horrified. How could this be possible? Was everything that he had worked so hard to achieve to be thrown in his face by his own dearly beloved grandchild?

Then he had had a dream, a dream in which a magician appeared to him and showed him how, despite her exile, Ruby's work had enabled the Land to flourish. Its economy had been about to crumble when, as if by magic, the much-anticipated tourists had finally begun to arrive on lightweight carts made of ash that traversed the roads as speedily as if they had wings.

And as the dream ended, the magician had told him that another magician would soon visit and would bring the Bureaucrat-in-Chief a very important message. When he awoke, he had glimpsed, from the corner of his eye, a small albino mouse perched on the bedstead. The tiny white mouse looked at him fixedly and then, if he was not mistaken, gave him a rather saucy wink before disappearing underneath the chest of drawers.

"Bloody mice," the Bureaucrat-in-Chief complained aloud. "I have passed several laws banning the nasty creatures and they just won't go away." He had not bothered creating any more laws for several years; it was getting so tedious, trying to keep track of them and the reference books of laws that were published annually had become so vast and so heavy that nobody was even able to lift them.

Ruby was very nervous about visiting the Land. She had been so young when she left, not much more than a girl. And now here she was, with silver threads beginning to appear at her temples and wrinkles around her eyes, preparing for the marriage of her only son to the granddaughter of the man whom she had always feared and hated with all her heart. It was with immense trepidation that she boarded the cart and headed home for the first time in so many years.

When Ruby and Grace arrived, they made their way first to the Palace to see the Bureaucrat-in-Chief. "Let's get it over with," Ruby said. "This won't be pleasant…"

The Palace was still large, yet it was no longer very magnificent. The gilt had been stripped from the towers and turrets to pay for the many debts that the Land had mounted up, the peacocks - so expensive to maintain and so exceptionally dim-witted and vain - were long gone, and most of the Palace had been closed for many years, as there were no guests to entertain in its vast rooms and no effective way of heating the long, echoing corridors. The only used quarters were those of the wing to which the Bureaucrat-in-Chief had retreated and now lived.

When Ruby and Grace approached the old man, who now sat before them in a rather ordinary armchair, he felt their faces carefully with his fingertips, as he was now blind. As his fingers traced their way across Ruby's face, he cried.

"Forgive me, my dear," he said. "I have done you a terrible wrong and I can see that now."

"I forgive you," Ruby said, realising, suddenly, that with her forgiveness she had suddenly let go of all her suffering about the matter. "It's over." Ruby smiled broadly as she realised the truth of her own words.

Then the old man turned to Grace. His fingers moved across her face and then stopped. "Wait," he said. "Are you not Grace?"

Ruby looked up in surprise. What was this?

"Yes, big brother," Grace whispered. "It is me."

"I thought you had drowned! When I pushed you, and you fell…"

"No, I was always a very strong swimmer."

"It was an accident, you know. I never meant to hurt you. And although I never confessed that it was because of me that the water swept you away, I have always blamed myself and done my best to stop such a thing happening to anyone else."

"I know. In a strange way, it was the best thing that could have happened. For had I not been picked up by a ship that day, I would never have travelled to see the world and I would never have learned all I know today."

"And are you still…?"

"Yes, Neville. I'm still a magician. I always will be."

"And the…"

"Yes. The albino mice. I still have them. It's all right; I don't expect you to understand. I have never been able to figure out their significance myself. I just know that it's part of the magic." As she said this, a small pair of bright eyes peeked out of her pocket and then quickly withdrew.

A year later, a baby girl was born to Peter and Orna and a naming ceremony was held in the Land. They decided to call her "Grace," a name that honoured

Ruby's closest friend and united their families. After the ceremony, Ruby picked up the little girl and brought her to the Bureaucrat-in-Chief. Although he was blind, his arms were still strong and he took the child without hesitation.

Smoothing the hair from the baby's forehead, the old man began to speak:

***

This story did not take place today or yesterday; it took place a long time ago when the animals still knew how to speak and before the stars had stopped singing. It was a village not very unlike this one and the times were very hard. Famine ravaged the land and many families did not have enough to eat. The men tightened their belts, the women adjusted their skirts and the children sucked on their leather mittens. Winter was coming in and people were staying in their own homes, counting out their beans and hoping and praying that they would live to see the spring...

***

And the baby smiled.

Lessons from The Circle Closes

One of my favourite words in the English language is "serendipity," though few people understand what it really means. It was coined by the English author Horace Walpole, who wrote in a letter of January 28, 1754, that "this discovery, indeed, is almost of that kind which I call serendipity, a very expressive word." The word had been formed from an early name for the country Sri Lanka, "Serendip," and he explained that the name in turn derived from a fairy story about the "Three Princes of Serendip" who, as they travelled, kept accidentally discovering things that they not even been searching for.

To many people, serendipity seems to be quite random. The truth is that through keen judgement, networking and awareness one creates many more opportunities for serendipitous things to happen. This is the spice that is the real difference between mere competence and excellence in business or in other endeavours. When you extend your awareness and are completely present, opportunities that would otherwise be passed by become real, tangible benefits that enrich your life. Make sure that you put yourself in the way of many opportunities and stay present and aware even when you are focussed on something else and you will stand a much greater chance of success.

A RECIPE FOR STONE SOUP

One generous portion of belief

One or more enthusiastic catalysts

One well defined context, communicated well

Testing for bad eggs so that you can leave them out

A heaping spoonful of emotion and trust

The ability to react proportionately and
level-headedly in times of crisis or change

A triple dose of reality

A preheated holistic present

A substantial dollop of perspective

A variety of questions including
self-questioning without self-doubt

Several spoonfuls of leadership
gravitas steeped in female energy

A large measure of inspiration fortified by deep listening

An embrace of change

A view of the bigger picture

Patience and presence

Effectual reasoning

Determination

An understanding that perception
is mutable and reality is not

Strategic insight

Personal and group goals created, shared and honoured

An embrace of the evolutionary
and iterative processes of change

Integrity

Disciplined, diligent practice

A pinch of serendipity

There are many kinds of listening, most of which are not listening at all. For example, there is distracted listening, there is listening to humour someone, there is listening for the gap in the conversation so that you can have your say, there is listening to judge or evaluate, there is listening to repeat and, finally, there is listening to understand. Nearly all the listening we do as humans can be categorised as one of these types, yet none of these are really powerful listening. Even when people practice so called active listening, if they also fall into one of the above-mentioned categories, then are they are not really listening at all, although the last two can sometimes approach real listening. In a world where nearly no one listens, is it any wonder that our species has the issues that it does?

Most people listen to their thoughts and the voices of doubt in their heads rather than listening to either the situation they are in or the person or people they are with. Some manage to briefly transcend their judgements and assessments in order to understand what they are hearing. A rare few listen closely to what others say and really understand what is being discussed. Fewer still listen to the whole context, searching for understanding rather than being distracted by their immediate needs and agenda. The most powerful people I know instinctively practice re-creative listening. They listen to everything that is there and that is not there in order to be able to fully recreate the experience of the speaker in their own body. This requires a stillness of mind and the ability to set aside the ego and temporarily suspend one's judgements, as well as the ability to direct one's awareness from within the mind to without, into the world.

The more re-creative listening is practiced, the more it can be sustained. We have all experienced flashes of pure clarity when we have grasped not just what someone is saying, when we have grasped and recreated for ourselves the very essence of what that person's life is like for them, including the context in which they are operating. This type of listening takes a great deal of effort and discipline to sustain. Despite this effort, it is very much worth practicing. Ironically, it is the least costly thing to do, in respect of the rewards it offers.

Anyone can listen re-creatively. If you choose to, you will need to enable yourself to do the following:

1. Silence your mind.

2. Extend your awareness outward.

3. Stay in the questions: "What is being said? What is missing? What more is there to come?"

By doing the above as often as you can in as many situations as possible, you will find yourself better able to understand and connect with the people you meet. You will be able to listen people into and out of things, just as you might talk someone into or out of something. While this sounds strange, I use this effect frequently. I truly believe that listening is the most important element of my own success. Without it, I am unable to contribute anything.

A RECIPE FOR STONE SOUP

One generous portion of belief

One or more enthusiastic catalysts

One well defined context, communicated well

Testing for bad eggs so that you can leave them out

A heaping spoonful of emotion and trust

The ability to react proportionately and
level-headedly in times of crisis or change

A triple dose of reality

A preheated holistic present

A substantial dollop of perspective

A variety of questions including
self-questioning without self-doubt

Several spoonfuls of leadership
gravitas steeped in female energy

A large measure of inspiration fortified by deep listening

An embrace of change

A view of the bigger picture

Patience and presence

Effectual reasoning

Determination

An understanding that perception
is mutable and reality is not

Strategic insight

Personal and group goals created, shared and honoured

An embrace of the evolutionary
and iterative processes of change

Integrity

Disciplined, diligent practice

A pinch of serendipity

Skilled and practiced listening

The Circle Closes

CHAPTER EIGHT

Be The Chef...
A Recipe for Success

*I once heard a young businessman
ask the Dalai Lama, "Where is the room
for spirituality in business?" As the room
went silent and I held my breath, The
Dalai Lama paused and then he chuckled
as he responded to the arrogant young
man by pronouncing, "Business people,
human beings too."*
Bill Liao, www.stonesoupway.com

S uccess does not have to mean to the same thing to
everyone. In fact, what a boring world it would be if
we all aimed for identical goals. Can you imagine?
What is more, "success" does not have to mean the same
thing for us at each stage of life. As in Ruby's case, our
aspirations at twenty do not have to be the same as our
aspirations at thirty, forty, fifty or beyond. What is
important is always to have a goal or goals and to work
towards them tirelessly. Success in its various guises can
be accessed by anyone who aims for it, works towards it,
and recognises where their input matters and where they
need the assistance or expertise of others.

We can all cook up our own recipe for success. We
can all make Stone Soup. This simple truth has never
been expressed to me more clearly than by a woman I

met in Uganda a few years ago. With her head held high, this woman proudly told me how she had sent a United Nations aid convoy on its way to bring its free food to those who needed it, because the community in which she worked had put aside enough food to take care of themselves and no longer required a hand-out. This was a community that, three years before, had been rife with poverty and destitution, not unlike the community outside the convent where Ruby paused for a year. People had been literally dying of hunger. Working together, the women and men of the village had changed everything, most especially their ability to rely on each other in tough times.

People often ask the question, "Which came first, the chicken or the egg?" In business and other forms of enterprise, the chicken-and-egg dilemma is a common riddle that many struggle to decipher. Let's suppose that Louis wants to start a company. He is likely to quickly run into a chicken-and-egg situation. Without money, he can't produce anything, and without products, he can't generate any income. From this starting point, Louis has to somehow manage to create something that he will then sell to customers he has not yet found. If he focuses on the obvious - that he has no money with which to produce the as yet merely imagined product - he is likely to stay stuck in the mud. Louis needs to start thinking in a new, fresh way if he is going to get his new enterprise off the ground. In fact, anyone who really wants to do something new and exciting in any field needs to become able to stop worrying about chickens and eggs and even omelettes and prepare to do what it takes to get all the ingredients together to make a really great batch of Stone Soup!

For Louis, as well as anyone interested in starting a new venture, the most important thing he can do right now is listen to everything and everyone around him, understanding that the world that we all share is a vast network of conversations. There is a lot to be learned. Of course, it is also extremely important to listen critically, because not all the information and opinions out there will necessarily be helpful.

The next step is to become able to articulate what the new business or enterprise is, clearly, succinctly and with the kind of avid ardour and passion one might reserve for one's first born child or an especially delicious chocolate gateau or perhaps one's favourite football team in the moments before, during and after the winning tiebreaker of the penalty shootout. Seriously; the succinctness of your articulation of the value that your enterprise generates and your level of enthusiasm are in direct proportion to the wildness of your future success.

Step three is to share and tune your vision to everyone who will listen until everyone you discuss it with is almost as excited about it as you are. In the process, the story or narrative of your enterprise will have been perfected. Don't worry about making your vision wholly unique; we all have a lot to learn from successful work that others have already done or are doing.

Step four is put together the goals of the business in a balanced way and then schedule them into a ninety-nine day plan so that you have a very clear course to share with everyone. Goals are opportunities to succeed or fail: either way, if you are smart you will make great progress and learn from your failures.

Step five is to gather your team together based on your plan, your goals and your passion. Do not collect team members who want you to give them something before they have proved themselves. People like that belong in established corporations or enterprises and don't fit in well with something new.

Step six: work. Work harder than you have ever imagined possible. If you are in business, be prepared to sacrifice the next three years of your life totally to it. If your involvement is in community activism, understand that your free time is largely a thing of the past. Your passion allows you to work so hard and that hard work is very attractive to others.

Throughout this process, remember that you are the leader. This is your vision and your narrative and that means that you are the leader of the team. That said, your job is mainly to build and inspire your team and everyone else with your vision; a vision that was not going to just happen by itself. Realise that the best leaders are not doing it themselves; they have great teams who can manage without them and yet would not be inspired to do so without leadership. The best leaders also have the very best advisers, so put together an advisory board that meets once a quarter. Make the board as large as you can and stuff it with the best people possible. Make sure your advisers challenge you and push them to look for the unintended consequences of what you do. Banning swimming caused John to drown. In the real world, drilling water bores in parts of India poisoned thousands with arsenic-contaminated deep water all in the name of common good. Make sure your advisers have made plenty of mistakes, so they can keep you from repeating them.

Whether your particular form of leadership is manifested in business, in your parent/teacher organisation or in an aid organisation or NGO, remember, above all, that the cure for chicken and egg syndrome is a hot bowl of nutritious Stone Soup made with love. Fortunately, from Ruby we've acquired a fantastic recipe for Stone Soup that is a great starting point for anyone eager to put their own stamp on it.

Stone Soup

ONE GENEROUS PORTION OF BELIEF

People often ask me: "If I want to invest in a business, what is the most important thing?" or "If I really want to make a difference in my community, how can I do it?" The answer is always the same: Enthusiasm.

Where does this celebrated enthusiasm come from and how can you get your hands on it? Enthusiasm comes from within and is often triggered by a passion (sometimes one you never knew you had). It is only generated when you believe in something and it is easier to share your belief if you can tell a story about it. You need to be able to build a narrative about what you want to do and where you are going. You need to become a storyteller, with your enterprise as protagonist and you as the raconteur who makes it all come real to anyone who listens. The more people who see the light in your eyes and are caught up in the story you tell about the little start-up that could, or the local community garden that blossomed, or the international movement for peace that really made a difference, the better the odds that real success will in fact be accomplished.

ONE OR MORE ENTHUSIASTIC CATALYSTS

Every enterprise, of whatever dimensions, needs catalysts. Catalysts are the people who facilitate action and make things happen. Of course, one of these catalysts needs to be you! In any type of organisation, the best resource you can have is your team of people and you want people to make things happen. These are women and men who have a reputation for getting things done; who can get in with other people and help you to bring them into the fold. Whether their personal skills are accounting or science or engineering doesn't matter; it's all about attitude and people skills. You particularly want to start with people who believe your story and with whom you get along well. Whatever you need to achieve, you've got to have enough people around you that want to get things done and will go out there and find the other people to bring in to you so that you can all work together.

You also need a variety of people. In Malcolm Gladwell's book, *The Tipping Point*, he mentions connectors, people who seem to know just about everyone in a certain field and mavens, people who seem to know just about everything on a certain topic. These types of people are important to any organisation. Of course, you will also need catalysts, and the majority of your team should be obsessed with execution. As I noted previously, great software companies have many more engineers than any other type of employee. They usually have one or two extraordinary engineers who are also business-and-people-savvy. At XING, our outsourcing development firm, Epublica, had a unique combination of founder programmers with these skills.

A CLEAR CONTEXT, COMMUNICATED WELL

There is no point speaking ancient Greek unless your target audience is ancient Greek scholars. If a message is worth communicating, it is worth communicating clearly, without confusing people with long words and esoteric concepts or jargon. Good ideas are at their strongest when they can be expressed in ways that people can understand, get into and begin to live.

TESTING FOR BAD EGGS SO
THAT YOU CAN LEAVE THEM OUT

When starting any new enterprise, one of the key chores is finding out which components are key to its success and which should be taken out. Remember: more ingredients do not necessarily result in better soup. Know what and who your organisation needs, and what and who it doesn't! Have no fear of getting rid of anything or anyone who is not going to be a massive contribution to success. Even very likable non-contributors unfairly drag down everything else and are better off left out.

A HEAPING SPOONFUL
OF EMOTION AND TRUST

If you read business texts from the 1950's you will see the often-repeated line that business is all about numbers and that the important thing is for the numbers to stack up and make sense. Truthfully, however, businesses and other organisations are all about emotion. If you, your customers and your team don't get moved by what you do, you might as well not be doing it. Know how to use emotion and how to make people understand that they can trust you or design things such that you earn trust quickly with little pain. At the same time, know that you need to be able to put yourself in a situation whereby you can trust them enough to disclose your emotions to them. If this doesn't seem possible, there's something seriously wrong.

THE ABILITY TO REACT PROPORTIONATELY & LEVEL-HEADEDLY IN TIMES OF CRISIS OR CHANGE

While there needs to be some drama in the story of your business, you do need to learn how to calibrate your reactions so that responses are proportionate to the reality of what is happening. Over-reactions will leach the energy and force you need to steer your business in the right direction, while under-reacting takes your eyes off the ball. Even when an organisation grows in strength and scope very quickly, there has to be a balance. It will take practice to find it and the balance will change, so it is important to always keep practicing. Never fear, though. By keeping up an open dialogue with your team and by trying different approaches you will get there. Just make sure that if you repeat the same thing three times without success you change it around before the fourth try.

A TRIPLE DOSE OF REALITY

Any new enterprise creates a new reality that is constantly regenerated as it is executed. Execution is all about doing something, measuring, seeing if it achieves what you said it was going to and, if it doesn't, redoing it until it does, because you have to deliver on your promises. People who really deliver what they say they will - be it profit for their company or a new support network for the vulnerable members of their community - are the entrepreneurs of their field. Those who don't produce any reality or changes to reality are mere dreamers. It has been written that entrepreneurs take risks. I disagree. I see that entrepreneurs manage their risks by understanding them well, by listening and communicating well, and by simply working their butts off to make up any shortfall.

A PREHEATED HOLISTIC PRESENT

What is a holistic present? It is a present that has absorbed the lessons of the past, while keeping a mindful eye on future goals. In any enterprise, it is crucial to have an understanding of where you are, where you came from and where you want to go. Dreadful mistakes are made by thinking things like, "That is how is has always been done, so I will do it like that too," or "There's always time tomorrow to get the details right," or saying to yourself, "I'll never do that again!" and then repeating the same thing days later.

You have to be able to live in the present and yet have both your past and your future available to you as a resource and ready reference if you are going to create a new business, or achieve anything at all. Basically, if we consider only the present we miss the future implications of what we do (and the possible unintended consequences). If we are obsessed with the past, we can't get anything done because we are obsessed with what has gone before and ways of doing things that may be obsolete. You've got to actually live the now to fulfil a future. You need to develop a planning tool that says: "This is how it is right now and the future I create means my actions right now are going to be a certain way. Here is the direction that we have got to take to reconcile future goals, present awareness and the foundation of the past." Over the years, I have seen too many entrepreneur hopefuls go out there and say, "Right, we can always be better tomorrow," while forgetting to work on today.

A SUBSTANTIAL DOLLOP OF FRESH PERSPECTIVE

How to know if your product, service or community work is actually going to do what it says on the tin? It is always a good idea to ask someone else. If you want to find out if something is going to be fun, ask someone who is doing it already. If you want to find out whether what you are doing is any good, rely on asking your customers to tell you; don't imagine it yourself. Look at the example of Ben and Jerry's Ice Cream. When they started out in business, Ben and Jerry asked just one marketing question. Doling out ice cream from their converted gas station, they asked of each new ice cream flavour: "Is it fun?" If it was fun, they kept the flavour and if it wasn't fun, they didn't. The most successful ice cream brand grew out of a simple question about others' perspectives: Is it fun?

A VARIETY OF QUESTIONS, INCLUDING SELF-QUESTIONING WITHOUT SELF-DOUBT

If you want to understand someone, ask them about where they grew up and what it was like growing up there and be prepared to listen to their answers. In general, you will get more information by asking questions and you will convince people more by asking questions than anything else you can do. All questions should be framed positively. Negative questioning is unproductive, dominant behaviour designed to make you feel right or others feel wrong. When you do either, you lose your connection to people and this is why resolutely positive questioning is so important.

SEVERAL SPOONFULS OF LEADERSHIP GRAVITAS STEEPED IN FEMALE ENERGY

Our world contains men and women, yet business and many other forms of enterprise feature masculine energy much more prominently than feminine. Male energy tends to be more about cutting things into pieces, building campaigns and deconstructing than female energy, which is more holistic and nurturing. As a leader - whether you are male or female - you will need to be able to tap into your personal reserves of female energy to grow your team and your enterprise. Society has changed immensely since the 1950's and old forms of leadership no longer work particularly well. Take on the responsibility and gravitas of leadership and do it in a way that encompasses traditional female skills of nurturing and seeing the bigger picture.

A LARGE MEASURE OF INSPIRATION
FORTIFIED BY DEEP LISTENING

True leaders are inspiring, and without that inspiration - that ability to help others to live the dream – there is no real enterprise. The more you become able to inspire people, the more people who believe in what you are doing, the more powerful your enterprise will be. At the same time, you have to listen, and I don't just mean any old kind of listening. I mean deep, creative listening to create something. Listening so that the person who is talking really feels heard as never before. Few things are more inspiring than knowing that one's concerns and interests are being listened to and taken on board.

AN EMBRACE OF CHANGE

As organisations or enterprises grow, they change and so do all the people involved in them. By failing to embrace change and work with a new set of circumstances instead of the old ones, we miss wonderful opportunities. People's capacity to change is astonishing. I have seen incredible things, such as the most nerdy programmer suddenly turn into the company's best salesperson because, all of a sudden, they have realised how to deal with people and they can now combine that skill with their knowledge of the product.

A View of the Bigger Picture

True leaders have a built-in zoom lens. They can zoom in to look at the details when and as necessary, and they can zoom way out to see the bigger picture. This ability is especially important during the first three years of an enterprise's existence, when it is essential to know every little detail of what is going on and just as important to understand how all those little details fit in overall. While truly great leaders don't get caught in the details, they can zoom down to understand them and use this ability to assist any member of their organisation to overcome a problem at their level.

Patience and Persistence

Both patience and persistence are prerequisites to success. It takes three years to grow a business. Most people don't have patience beyond three days. This is something that will have to change if they want to make their enterprise work. Think of all the patience that is required: you have to be patient with your people, your suppliers, your customers and with everyone else, while maintaining your grip on enough impatience to keep things moving along. That impatience will help to drive persistence. One needs to be always pushing to find a solution to every challenge and an opportunity in every difficulty. In my experience, there is always a way through. There is always an answer, so long as you keep pushing.

Effectual Reasoning

A lot of people use their powers of reason to set up tasks that have no real point or purpose in the greater scheme of things. Effectual reasoning forgets about clever games with logic and focuses instead on doing what needs to be done. Think in terms of how to get from A to B in the quickest, most effective way. Think of the impact of what you are doing. Think of the effect, rather than some grandiose theory.

DETERMINATION

People often think that persistence and determination are the same thing. They are not. Determination is about knowing that you can determine your future; that you have the power in your hands. When you create your plan, it is a future that you have created, that you have determined. That you can speak your word and, in the words of Jean Luc Picard, "Make it so!"

AN UNDERSTANDING THAT PERCEPTION IS MUTABLE AND REALITY IS NOT

How you, your customers, and the world, perceive something can be changed. Reality rarely can, especially past reality. Think about being slapped in the face. That's reality. Now think about how you will feel depending on who slaps you: a jilted lover, a parent, a small child, a random person on the street. That is perception.

STRATEGIC INSIGHT

When you look at something and gain an insight that you hadn't had before, it is often tremendous. Yet what is a useful insight? I've seen people look at something and catalogue what's there without actually spending time thinking, "What is missing? If I had that thing, would we get where we are going? What is the one thing that I could possess that would change this?" That is a strategic insight: looking - or hunting - for the thing that you need to get rid of, or that is missing, that will then lead you to your goal.

PERSONAL AND GROUP GOALS:
CREATED, SHARED & HONOURED

The most important factor of success is having goals. Without goals that are shared, goals that are lined up, measurable and in a hierarchy of importance, you might as well forget about whatever it is you want to do. It is immensely important to make your goals known, to share them with everybody and to let everyone know how you are working towards them, to help them understand what you are doing. Also, by sharing your goals, you will also figure out pretty quickly if the people you are working with share your worldview, principles, and vision. I actually divide my goals up into the ones for myself, my company, my customers, and the rest of the world. I also divide them up according to whether they are open-ended or closed and measurable, and I rank then in a hierarchy (with open, philanthropic ones on top) and I share them. This process gets me and everyone around me very clear on what we are all doing and what makes us do it and what to choose to do next.

Embracing the Evolutionary and Iterative Processes

Things change, often radically and rarely how one expects them to. Some of the most successful businesses in the world started out doing one thing, and are now doing something completely different. Look at American Express - it started as a stagecoach company and now it is a credit card company. Amazing things happen when you create a model that can evolve. I've seen this happen in my experience, too. When we first launched XING, it was terrible! What made it good was the fact that we were able to change it and take all the user feedback that we were getting to make each new generation a little better than the one before. In ninety days, we were profitable.

INTEGRITY

Integrity is all about giving your word and honouring it – this is extraordinarily important. Without integrity, nothing worthwhile gets done, because integrity makes things workable. More than keeping one's word, integrity is about always striving to do so and apologising and making things right when that doesn't happen. Surveys on customer satisfaction show that businesses that occasionally deliver faulty goods or services and then do their courteous utmost to make things right as quickly and efficiently as possible leave customers feeling as good as if everything had gone perfectly smoothly in the first instance - often better.

GENEROSITY

My grandfather used to say, "There's got to be beer enough for both of us."

Generosity is a two way street. The more you give, the more you will get back in return. When you give extraordinary value - beyond that which is expected - it is amazing what you will be given in return. I am not just talking about money; I am talking about reputation, ideas and loyalty. When you give to a customer beyond all expectation, you will often receive undying loyalty in return. All businesses, organisations and charities should display great generosity of spirit. Give you and will receive.

DISCIPLINED DILIGENT PRACTICE

Anyone who wants to be world class has to practice, practice and practice. It takes time and effort to make lasting achievement. In my experience, I know that I am good at listening. I was not born with a magical gift; I have put in the time to learn how to listen long, carefully and well, and take a great deal from what I hear. Of course, in order to work that hard at learning something, it is necessary to love what you do, to care about it and to be inspired every day by each little step along the way.

A PINCH OF SERENDIPITY

"Serendipity" is my favourite word in the English language and to show you why, I will tell you a little story. During the writing of this book, I found myself waiting in Paddington Station in London. I was having a snack in Yo Sushi!, a sushi franchise, when I noticed an older gentleman, quintessentially English in his Yorkshire check hat, wearing an Asian jacket and eating sushi enthusiastically with a pair of chopsticks. He made such a perfect picture, I asked if I could take his photograph (which I subsequently titled "Serendipity" and posted on Flickr). Afterwards we got to talking and I found out that this gentleman was writing a book about trees and was involved with the Prince's Trust. His environmental interests fitted perfectly with mine at weforest.com and soon we had even planned to do some work together. All of this from a completely random meeting between two people who just happened to be open-minded enough to strike up conversation in a railway eatery!

SKILLED AND PRACTICED LISTENING

If you are thinking that I might have mentioned this before, well, I have, and more than once. And that's because listening - really, seriously listening - is the most important thing of all. Most people listen only waiting for their turn to speak, or they listen patronisingly or, worse still, they try to judge and listen at the same time. In conversation, the person you are engaging with needs to feel listened to. It is easy to tell when someone is really listening, because their body language speaks loud and clear. Even when it is your turn to speak, you need to be listening to the other side to see if your message is getting across. I am not talking about listening to judge here. I am talking about listening to achieve, active listening first, asking questions and then recreating in yourself how it is for the person you are listening to without judging (you can always judge later). You listen with an intention that has been stated. Listening deeply without judging while still holding an intention can be truly transformative.

Listening to create is the most powerful tool that I have ever had in business or any other endeavour and it takes some practice. If an idea sounds fuzzy when you first listen to someone, assume it's because you have not really listened first. In Alan Webber's book, *52 Principles for Winning at Business Without Losing Your Self*[13], I am quoted as saying "Connectedness is effectiveness." I continue to stand by that simple rule. And at bottom, being connected - really connected - is all about knowing how to listen.

---

[13] Webber, 2009, p. 261.

CHAPTER NINE

Be It

I hope that you have enjoyed accompanying me on Ruby's journey, and that the various things that we have learned along the way will help all you be the best you can possibly be. Remember: you have the power to change the world and your place in it for the better! And remember, too, that every great recipe can deal with the contents of the individual chef's kitchen cabinets. Use the recipe here and make your own soup extra-special with those added ingredients seasoned with the love and passion that can only come from you!

Bon appétit.

Afterword

As you've reached this point, I'm sure that you've been very impressed by the powerful lessons contained in Bill Liao's Stone Soup.

Having also read about Ruby's journey, what is most inspiring and empowering to me is Bill's embrace of the power and vitality of women and girls in combination with that of their fathers and brothers. As an international women's rights activist, I'm very sensitive to how often females are often completely left out. We are not consulted, let alone asked to participate with our particular views of the world. It's taken decades for international aid organisations to finally realise, for instance, that 80% of the farmers in sub-Saharan Africa are female and yet, they have no say in agricultural policy. A majority of war refugees are women and children, and yet mothers are not included at the negotiation tables when it comes to war or peace. Gandhi is credited with the adage, "Educate a man, you educate an individual; educate a woman, you educate a family". Many people have noted that when a woman learns to read, she teaches all her children to read, not just the boys. Women and girls are missing from all sorts of tables: board rooms, governments and domestic tables for basic meals, since a majority of the world's under-nourished are women and girls. They are expected to grow, gather, prepare and serve, but not necessarily partake equally in nourishment.

Yet time and time again, when women – not just one woman as a token - are included with men in decision-making and problem solving, the entire family, society and country benefit. Bill Liao knows this and stands by half the world's population in being necessary for transformation of the human family and its precious home, earth.

Ellen Snortland, www.snortland.com

About Bill Liao

Bill Liao, high school drop-out, multi-millionaire businessman and social entrepreneur is co-founder of the social network service XING. Bill is European Venture Partner with SOSventures, working with Sean O'Sullivan to invest in world changing companies. He is also the co-founder of CoderDojo a global collaboration to provide free learning for young people to develop the ability to program computers and write software.

Among his philanthropic endeavours is his participation as an investor and volunteer in The Hunger Project in Uganda, New York and Mexico.

Bill has also been appointed as a special diplomatic envoy for St Kitts and Nevis for sustainable development and the environment. Bill has contributed to the St Kitts and Nevis recovery fund for the sugar cane industry there.

In 2007, Bill founded neo.org, a philanthropic venture and social networking site where people can make a personal commitment for the future of the earth. Neo is an international non-profit organisation based in Switzerland and supported by a team of individuals from across the globe. It was set up to provide a forum for people to make a personal commitment for the future of the earth in the form of a Declaration of Global Citizenship.

In 2009, Bill also founded www.weforest.com, an organisation dedicated to repairing the world through the permaculture reforestation of 20 million square kilometres of land by 2020.

Originally from Australia, Bill, his wife Kerrie and their three children, Liam, Riley and Willow, live in the mountains of Switzerland together with their numerous animals.

References

Bartley, William Warren, Werner Erhard The Transformation of a Man: The Founding of EST, Clarkson Potter, 1988

Becker, Gavin De & Snortland, Ellen B. Beauty Bites Beast: Awakening the Warrior Within Women and Girls, B3 Books, 2001

Block, P, Community: the Structure of Belonging, Barrett-Koehler, 2008

Brafman, Ori and Beckstrom, Rod. The Starfish and the Spider: The Unstoppable Power of Leaderless Organizations, Penguin (October 5, 2006), Burke, K, Language as symbolic action, Berkley & Los Angeles: University of California Press, 1966

Coyle, Daniel, The Talent Code, Bantam, 2009

Davenport, TH; Beck, JC, The Attention Economy: Understanding the New Currency of Business, Harvard Business School Press, 2001

Diamond, Jared, Collapse: How Societies Choose to Fail or Succeed, New York: Viking Books, 2005

Eisenberg, B; Eisenberg J, Davis, L, Waiting for your Cat to Bark? Persuading Customers when they Ignore Marketing, Thomas Nelson, 2006

Erhard, W Jensen, MC, Zaffron, S, Integrity: Where Leadership Begins - A New Model of Integrity (PDF File of PowerPoint Slides) Barbados Group Working Paper No. 07-03, Harvard NOM Working Paper No. 07-03 Independent , Harvard Business School and Vanto Group

Gall, John, Systemantics: The Underground Text of Systems Lore, How Systems Really Work and How They Fail (Second Edition), General Systemantics Press, 1986

Gilbert, D, Stumbling on Happiness, Vintage, 2007

Gladwell, Malcolm, The Tipping Point: How Little Things Can Make a Big Difference, Back Day Books, 2002

Hecke, Margaret, Blind Spots: Why Smart People Do Dumb Things. Prometheus Books, 2007

Kristof, Nicholas D, WuDunn, Sheryl, The Women's Crusade, New York Times Magazine, August 9th, 2009

Manjoo, Farhad, True Enough, Learning to Live in a Post Fact Society, Wiley, 2008

Pease, A; Pease B, Why Men Don't Listen and Women Can't Read Maps: How We're Different and What to Do About It, Broadway, 2001

Pease, A; Pease, B, Why Men Lie and Women Cry, Manjul Publishing House Pvt Ltd, 2006

Sarasvathy, Sara, What Makes Entrepreneurs Entrepreneurial? Available at SSRN: *http://ssrn.com/abstract=909038*

Strauss, N, The Game: Penetrating the Secret Society of Pick-up Artists, Morrow, 2006

Strayer, David; Drews, Frank; Crouch, Dennis (PDF), FATAL Distraction? A Comparison of The Cell-Phone Driver & The Drunk Driver, University of Utah Department of Psychology, *http://www.psych.utah.edu/AppliedCognitionLab/DrivingAssessment2003.pdf*

Van Hecke, M, Blind Spots, Why Smart People do Stupid Things, Prometheus, 2007

Webber, Alan, Rules of Thumb: 52 Principles for Winning at Business without Losing Your Self, Harper Business, 2009

Zimbardo, P and Boyd, J The Time Paradox: The New Psychology of Time That Will Change Your Life, Free Press, 2009

The Ultimate Recipe for Stone Soup

One generous portion of belief: believe in what you do!

One or more enthusiastic catalysts: great people make things happen!

A clear context communicated well: no talking without listening!

Testing for bad eggs so that you can leave them out:
assess what you need and what you don't!

A heaped spoonful of emotion, and one of trust:
feelings and principles are important!

The ability to react proportionately and level-
headedly to the things that happen: stay cool!

A triple measure of reality: know what matters!

A preheated holistic present: learn from the past,
create the future, live in the now that results!

A substantial dollop of fresh perspective: opinions count!

Positive self-questioning: query the status quo!

Several spoonfuls of leadership gravitas
steeped in female energy: lead and nurture!

A large measure of inspiration fortified
with deep listening: listen to inspire!

An embrace of change: don't stay stuck in the past!

A view of the bigger picture: know how to operate your zoom lens!

Patience and persistence: keep calm, keep busy!

Effectual reasoning: act your decisions!

Determination: see it through!

An understanding that perception is mutable and reality
is not: know what can be changed and what cannot!

Strategic insight: look, listen for what is missing and learn!

Create, share and honour your goals and
the goals of the group: live your goals!

Embracing the evolutionary and iterative
processes: accept the need to adapt!

Integrity: fulfil your promises!

Generosity: if you give, you get!

Disciplined diligent practice: practice until
you get it right, and then practice more!

A pinch of serendipity: you never know what might turn up!

Listening: keep listening, listening, listening!

One Page Business Plan

What extrinsic open goal for the world can our company take on?

_____

(Microsoft's extrinsic open goal was: "A computer on every desk.")

What three questions should we be asking all the time?

_____

(Yahoo had a key question, asked of everything they did: "Is it fast?")

What value do we create?

_____

(What will someone pay for?)

When will our company break even?

_____

(Be as simple as possible; answer this by multiplying cash per sale by the number of sales and subtracting all your costs.)

How will you grow profits without growing costs?

_____

(The more you can grow your profits without adding additional costs the better your business will be.)

How can I establish and maintain traction?

_____

(Traction is that point at which the business has become established and starts to develop momentum. Whether your enterprise is profit-oriented or voluntary, it has traction when the numbers using or engaging with it are growing steadily, and when they stay engaged rather than using it just once.)

Now imagine yourself wildly successful three years in the future. From there, look back and create a draft time line below. On the time line, list all the closed goals, with dates, that had to happen to get you the success you imagine. This is now your time plan. Revisit the time plan weekly to refine it and share it with your people often. Remember that only change is certain.

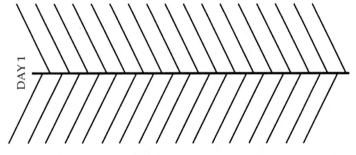

DAY 1

WEEK 36

CoderDojo

CoderDojo – a wonderful real-world example of Stone Soup in practice!

James Whelton, a young coder, started a computer club while he was still at secondary school. He had expertise, passion and time to share – and that was about all. Still, it's surprising how much can be achieved with just those three precious ingredients.

James had always loved coding and, like many budding geeks, taught himself in his bedroom. He won a web award and the school headmaster announced it over the PA. This one announcement caused kids across the school to seek him out to learn how he managed to get good at programming. James could see how many other kids were eager to get into the world of coding too. The problem was that they had few opportunities to engage with coders, while the linear world of the traditional classroom is not exactly the best environment in which to learn this particular skill. James started a computer club to help them. When James finished his Leaving Certificate he wanted to find a way to keep the club going.

In 2011 James met Bill, the author of this book. Bill had experience making scalable start-ups, and had also worked with charities like his own WeForest.org. When James told Bill the story of the club, what Bill immediately heard was that there was market demand from kids to learn how to code. With Bill as co-founder, they created CoderDojo, a new educational movement that provides a learning environment in which young people (and some older ones) are enabled to start coding in a collaborative, child-led learning environment.

James and Bill worked hard to create a story that could easily be retold and a brand that was cool as well as rules and curriculum. They came up with one rule: Be Cool. Then they decided to use their story to find a venue donor. The National Software Center and CORKBIC volunteered a room for free and the movement was born. A few months later, it had produced the first 12 year old, Harry Moran, to successfully launch a commercial app, PizzaBot, on the Apple app store.

CoderDojo borrows its educational philosophy from the teaching methods that have been utilised in the field of martial arts for over 2000 years. The movement is also completely free and no money changes hands. There isn't even a bank account. Spaces for learning are provided for free by a range of public and private bodies, and mentors and supervisors generously give their time on a voluntary basis. Guest lectures visit from some of the most cutting-edge areas of computer technology and robotics. Above all, the CoderDojo members bring their curious, open minds, optimism, creativity and willingness to embrace the new and often challenging.

The world's very first CoderDojo opened in a small town in Ireland at a time when the country (and much of the world, for that matter) was deep in recession. Within a year the movement had spread across Ireland, and had leapfrogged to locations as diverse as Italy, Japan, the United States and the United Kingdom, with more CoderDojos being formed every month. At the time of writing, thousands of young people get together every week to learn some of the world's most exciting new languages – and their numbers are growing exponentially.

Learning how to code is a lot more than just a fun hobby. Knowing coding languages is a new form of literacy and it empowers and enables creativity. Already, some of the coders who love CoderDojo have become involved in developing computer applications, some of which have become big sellers. Most importantly, the young people who participate in CoderDojo are helping to create a more connected world in which they will be enabled to make their voices heard on an international stage. They are true creators and not just users. They are global citizens.

A considerable body of evidence suggests that learning languages is best done at a young age in order to become a native speaker sufficiently adept to create poetry. Just as poets produce more impact with fewer words, so do great coders produce more impact with fewer lines of code. CoderDojo is teaching these languages at the right age, in a social and collaborative way that is much healthier than learning alone. Kids are empowered both to create and to play well with others.

The founders of CoderDojo envision a future in which there is a CoderDojo in every district in Ireland and all across the world, enabling future generations to communicate and learn as never before – and putting the principles of stone soup-making into action!

The model has proven to be so doable, perhaps you'll feel inspired to start a CoderDojo yourself. You can do this for free using the simple tools available on www.coderdojo.com

www.coderdojo.com

Lightning Source UK Ltd.
Milton Keynes UK
UKOW052016160113

204983UK00012B/682/P